Praise for

A CLIMATE FOR CHANGE

"Climate scientists are best able to tell us if, how, and why Earth's climate is changing. Ethicists and religious scholars and leaders are best able to tell us how we should respond to the knowledge that science provides. Authored by a climate scientist and a religious leader, this book provides a unique perspective on Christian responses to the findings of climate science. Anyone who is open to messages from both science and Christian Scriptures will be struck by the insight and synthesis of this remarkable author team. With clarity unusual in science reports and impeccable logic, A CLIMATE FOR CHANGE is a compelling call to action."

—James J. McCarthy, Agassiz
Professor of Oceanography, Harvard University, and
president of the American Association for
the Advancement of Science (2008)

"This is a book all Christians should read. It makes the science, the issues, and even the misunderstandings come alive. Christians need to help in the fight against climate change and its effects. Jesus calls Christians to serve 'the least of these'—the poor and oppressed of the developing world—who are most affected by climate change. This book is a compelling call to action for any Christian who cares about the issues our world is facing today. And that should be all of us."

—Dean Hirsch, president, World Vision International

a climate for change

global warming facts for
faith-based decisions

To Steve
from Kathy

KATHARINE HAYHOE

ANDREW FARLEY

Fodder for many more interesting
discussions with my dad!

Faith
Words

New York Boston Nashville

Scripture quotations marked NIV are taken from the HOLY BIBLE, NEW INTERNATIONAL VERSION®. Copyright © 1973, 1978, 1984 International Bible Society. Used by permission of Zondervan. All rights reserved. The "NIV" and "New International Version" trademarks are registered in the United States Patent and Trademark Office by International Bible Society. Use of either trademark requires the permission of International Bible Society.

Scripture quotations marked NLT are taken from the Holy Bible, New Living Translation, copyright 1996, 2004. Used by permission of Tyndale House Publishers, Inc., Wheaton, Illinois 60189. All rights reserved.

Scripture quotations marked NASB are taken from the NEW AMERICAN STANDARD BIBLE®. Copyright © 1960, 1962, 1963, 1968, 1971, 1972, 1973, 1975, 1977, 1995 by The Lockman Foundation. Used by permission.

Scripture quotations marked *The Message* are taken from *The Message*. Copyright © 1993, 1994, 1995, 1996, 2000, 2001, 2002. Used by permission of NavPress Publishing Group.

Scripture quotations noted TNIV are taken from the Holy Bible, Today's New International Version™ TNIV®. Copyright © 2001, 2005 by International Bible Society®. All rights reserved worldwide.

FaithWords
Hachette Book Group
237 Park Avenue
New York, NY 10017

Visit our website at www.faithwords.com.

Printed in the United States of America

First Edition: October 2009

10 9 8 7 6 5 4 3 2 1

FaithWords is a division of Hachette Book Group, Inc.
The FaithWords name and logo are trademarks of Hachette Book Group, Inc.

Library of Congress Cataloging-in-Publication Data

Hayhoe, Katharine.
    A climate for change : global warming facts for faith-based decisions / Katharine Hayhoe, Andrew Farley — 1st ed.
        p. cm.
    Includes bibliographical references.
    ISBN 978-0-446-54956-1
    1. Global warming—Religious aspects—Christianity.   I. Farley, Andrew.
II. Title.
    BR115.G58H38 2009
    261.8'8—dc22   2009013088

For anyone who has ever wondered whether climate change is real.

ACKNOWLEDGMENTS

We gratefully acknowledge the assistance of Clare Keating, Brittanie Lassiter, Jeff VanDorn, Deborah Padilla, Julia Verville, and Ximena Bernal in compiling all the information that went into this book. We also thank David Gerratt and Amanda Wait of DG Communications (NonprofitDesign.com) for their outstanding work in designing the figures center spread.

We extend our heartfelt thanks to the readers who forged their way through early drafts of this book and provided us with valuable comments and feedback, especially when it was "I have no idea what you're talking about here!" Among them are Kathy Beerbower, Leslie Farley, Linda Hendrickson, John McCuin, Jenny Strovas, Jeremy and Tessa Short, and Josh Sills. We also benefitted from early discussions at St. John's Methodist and Second Baptist Church, both in Lubbock, Texas.

We also want to thank Rasmus Benestad, Jessica Hellman, Peter Kareiva, Jeff Masters, Susanne Moser, Scott Sheridan, and Lew Ziska for their thoughtful insights; Nancy Cole and the Union of Concerned Scientists, and Emily Murgatroyd and the Desmogbloggers for their cheerful assistance; and Katharine's cousin Anita for always asking, "Why don't you just write a book?"

CONTENTS

Preface   xi

Introduction: Christians and Climate Change   xiii

part one
WHAT'S GOING ON?

1. The Kivalina Story	3
2. Our Changing Planet	8
3. Indicators of Change	15
4. Decisions and Consequences	21

part two
CAUSES

5. God's Gift: The Earth	29
6. The Natural Suspects	35
7. The Human Fingerprint	41
8. We've Done It Before	48

part three
DOUBTS

9. Weather Is Not Climate	55
10. The Natural Way of Things	60
11. No More Debate	67
12. A Window to Our Climate Future	74

part four
EFFECTS

13. Increasing Extremes   83

14. Water: Feast or Famine   89

15. On Thin Ice   96

16. Rising Seas   101

17. Our Fragile Food Chain   107

18. Squirrels and Seeds   113

part five
CHOICES

19. Motivation for Change   123

20. No Fear in Life   129

21. Spiritual Freedom, Wisdom, and Compassion   136

22. Small Steps Toward Change   141

23. Taking On the World   150

Epilogue   159

Further Reading   161

Discussion Questions   163

Sources   166

About the Authors   205

PREFACE

Bike to work. Hug a tree. Eat granola. Live off the grid. Wear hemp. Bathe in a stream. And worship the earth.

We often find ourselves labeled—just because we think global warming is a serious problem people should know about.

But here's who we really are.

We're Christians. We don't worship the earth. We worship the Creator of the universe. We believe that God spoke the world into existence and sustains it by His power. We believe that Jesus Christ is the way to eternal life, that the Bible is God's Word, and that nothing compares to the importance of the gospel message.

Now, for what we *don't* believe. We don't believe the universe came into existence through random chance. We don't believe that life came from nothing or that humans evolved from apes.

We don't believe in government running our lives or in destroying the economy to save the earth. We believe in common sense. We believe in the sensible progression from older to newer technologies.

Yes, we live in a house with air-conditioning. We drive cars. We don't have solar panels on our roof (too expensive), and we're not vegetarians (meat is just too tasty).

Don't worry—we're not going to try to convince you that Earth is four billion years old or that it's young, but with the appearance of age. Even we, the authors, disagree on that one.

Climate change is about thermometers and temperatures. It's about what's been happening on our planet since the Industrial Revolution. It's Chemistry 101.

Now, let's talk about global warming!

CHRISTIANS AND CLIMATE CHANGE

> "For most of us, until recently this has not been treated as a pressing issue or major priority. Indeed, many of us have required considerable convincing before becoming persuaded that climate change is a real problem and that it ought to matter to us as Christians."
>
> —*Climate Change: An Evangelical Call to Action*

The idea for this book developed slowly, over time. It grew out of questions we received from people trying to separate climate change fact from fiction. It came from conversations with friends who wanted to know the "truth" about climate change from a fellow Christian, someone they could trust. It was fed by discussions with colleagues, who wanted to understand the "religious position" on climate change from someone they knew was a Christian.

As we have listened to our friends, colleagues, and the people around us, we've realized we have an incredible opportunity to speak out on one of the most pressing issues facing our generation. Most Christians are not scientists, and it's hard to say how many scientists are Christians. In our family, we have both.

Katharine studies how climate change will affect the places we live. Andrew pastors a church in Texas where many Christians just don't buy into the whole global warming thing. Together, we have talked to Christians all over the country who are asking whether or not climate change is real. They want to know if it's a genuine crisis that requires our attention or if the whole thing is just a lot of smoke and mirrors. They also want to know what the Bible says, if anything, about a Christian response.

A Christian Perspective?

Even talking about climate change from a Christian perspective might seem suspect, because so many people associate global warming with a certain agenda. The issue just isn't on our collective radar of things Christians should be concerned about.

Common thought on climate change generally sounds something like this:

- How do we know that climate change is really happening?
- Wasn't there a record cold winter just last year in such-and-such a place?
- All those scientists are always disagreeing with each other.
- It's too early to decide—we just don't have enough information.

Some people who acknowledge that our climate *is* changing believe it's just another natural cycle that has nothing to do with human activity.

You may have heard others say something like: "Those save-the-whales, tree-hugging liberal activists are just pushing the human angle as part of their agenda to turn the world into a place where everyone eats raw vegetables and worships the mother goddess."

Or here's another view: "Even if it turns out that global warming is real, and we're somewhat to blame for it, there's nothing we can do without destroying our economy. It's much wiser just to wait it out. We've adapted successfully to everything nature has thrown at us so far. Why would this be any different? And we know from the Bible that the world doesn't end because of global warming. So what's the big deal?"

Still others might say that climate change *is* happening, that we *are* responsible, and that the effects are likely to be serious. But they might add, "All we really need to do is pray. If we have enough faith, we can move mountains, right? So we should just offer up some prayers and then get on with our lives."

A Sea of Opinions

As Christians, we're naturally suspicious of people who believe differently from us. How can such activists—those whose voices have so often been raised against us on fundamental issues like family and the sanctity of life—have anything worthwhile to say about the environment?

In the past, we may have seen climate change used as a political tool on the part of this party or that organization to manipulate and get what they want. Our hesitations are justified. It's hard to trust information from sources we feel might manipulate facts to suit their political agenda.

But the issue of climate change really is different. It's not about blue politics or red politics or any kind of politics. It's about thermometer readings and history. It's about facts and figures. It's about reality. And that's what we want to explore with you in this book.

Who's on board already? Is there any solid, reliable group that's already convinced that climate change is real? Well, yes, actually there is.

A recent report commissioned by the Pentagon concluded that abrupt changes in climate may be the greatest security threat we face in the twenty-first century. Eleven National Academies of Science, including that of the United States, signed a statement concluding that human-induced climate change is real and that world leaders need to take prompt action to reduce its causes. Industry leaders ranging from Wal-Mart to General Electric have called for national standards for reducing emissions of heat-trapping gases. Polls show that a growing number of registered Republican voters believe global warming will pose a serious threat within their lifetime. Republicans such as John McCain and Newt Gingrich have issued strong statements regarding the necessity for reducing our environmental impact on the planet. This last decade, we've seen a radical shift in the conservative mind-set.

The Christian community has similarly been galvanized by calls to action from prominent leaders. In 2006, the Evangelical Climate Initiative was released, which stated that our moral convictions as evangelicals demand a response to the climate change problem. The leaders of nearly one hundred churches, charities, and seminaries from the Salvation Army to Saddleback Church signed the initiative. In 2007, the U.S. Conference of Catholic Bishops announced that, by harming the atmosphere, a God-given gift that supports life here on Earth, we dishonor our Creator and His gift of creation.

In 2008, forty Southern Baptist leaders, a convention that traditionally sides with more conservative viewpoints, declared that we as Christians should take responsibility for our contributions to environmental issues. They stated that it's not only prudent, but also necessary, for individuals, churches, communities, and governments to act now to curb actions that are causing degradation of the environment. A survey of evangelical Christians the same year found that although less than a third were firmly convinced that global warming was happening, 45 percent had made recent changes to become more environmentally conscious, and 90 percent thought they should take a more active role in caring for creation.

Why this growing shift in opinion? We think it's because Christians are beginning to realize that climate change is really about physical changes that can have serious consequences on our lives. It's about temperature records and rainfall patterns, not liberals or conservatives. We've reached the point where we can no longer stand by, believing that climate change is the invention of some radical mastermind to push forward his or her political agenda. People of all political persuasions are now recognizing that climate change is real and it's happening now.

There are legitimate reasons why Christians have hesitated to take on the climate change concern. For example, doesn't climate change mean that we have to believe in evolution and a four-billion-year-old Earth? Not at all. Climate change is fully understandable without ascribing a birth date to planet Earth. As we go back in Earth's history, our satellite, thermometer, natural, and written records consistently validate the dramatic and unprecedented nature of the recent increase in heat-trapping gases in the atmosphere. And this recent increase corresponds directly with the dawn and growth of our industrial age less than three hundred years ago.

But what about natural cycles and the sun? Carbon dioxide from plants and volcanoes? Yes, we can account for these and many other frequently heard objections to the science of climate change.

This book, then, is an invitation. Find out more about the *why* of climate change and the truth about the most popular "spins" put on the issue. Climate change may not be obvious where you live, but real people around the world are being affected in drastic ways today. The impacts of climate change are already a reality.

Let's begin with a story about some real people whose lives are being threatened by climate change.

And they just happen to be Americans.

what's going on?

1

THE KIVALINA STORY

"For thousands of years, our people have survived in the Arctic simply by being aware of our surroundings. [Today] it is simply not safe for us to continue to live on the barrier reef. We need to move our village now."

—Colleen Swan, Tribal Administrator

Early on Easter morning, the sound of gospel music streams out across the frozen ocean some eighty miles north of the Arctic Circle. It's not what you'd expect to hear in this remote, snow-covered wilderness. But the Inupiaq people of Kivalina assemble to celebrate and sing on this, their most important holiday of the year. They've held vigil all night long to welcome the Resurrection Day.

About seventy homes are huddled together on a narrow six-hundred-foot-wide reef sandwiched between the Chukchi Sea and the Kivalina Lagoon. Just over four hundred people live here on the edge of the world. Today they've gathered to commemorate the most fundamental of Christian truths—the transformation of death into resurrected life. In this frigid north, the sun itself appears to celebrate as the days around Easter lengthen, transforming the Arctic from a world of darkness into one of light.

The Inupiaq people of northwest Alaska have lived along the frozen shores of the Chukchi Sea for generations. Over time, they've learned to adapt to harsh conditions and sustain their existence. Beluga and bowhead whales, ringed and bearded seals, fish, caribou, and polar bears provide their livelihood.

Originally, they lived inland in camps that allowed them freedom to move with the seasons and the availability of food. As the season for hunting whales gave way to the season for stalking caribou, the Inupiaq would move back and forth from the coast.

But everything changed in the early 1900s when a government ship arrived. The ship brought building materials for a new school. Unaware of the Inupiaq's back-and-forth seasonal travel from shore to inland, the workers aboard the ship simply dropped the supplies at the tip of the long barrier island. It was there, beside the shore, that the new school was built.

Shortly afterward, new laws were passed that required the Inupiaq to enroll their children in school. This legislation ultimately resulted in the construction of a permanent village, bravely poised between sea and river, where the land was just six hundred feet across at its widest point (see Figure 1 in the center insert).

Over the years, the village of Kivalina has survived many trials. In the 1950s, storm waves nearly overtopped the island. But these rare events were tolerable. As solutions to these trials, the Inupiaq preferred building seawalls or the occasional reconstruction project rather than uprooting the community. Until recently, that is.

A Village on the Edge

The idea of moving the town was first broached and voted down in the 1960s. Now, however, it appears to be the only option.

What used to be considered uncharacteristically early storms are now arriving year after year, pounding the island. Protective sea ice, which in the past has buffered the island from winter storms, has been forming later each year. In the early 1980s, the Inupiaq could usually plan for three months of ice-free conditions in summer before the autumn freeze. Now, ice-free conditions last up to five months each year. Fall storms strike before the ice forms, dragging foot after foot of loose sand into the hungry sea. This opens the island up to massive erosion and a host of other problems.

Compounding the concern is the island itself. It's formed of a combination of frozen ice and ground called *permafrost*. This foundation used to be as solid as cement. But in recent years, the permafrost has been melting and cracking. Large holes are opening up in the ground, and every time a storm hits, more ground washes into the sea. During a single fall storm season in 2004, Colleen Swan, the tribal administrator, estimates that the town lost sixty feet of coastline. The school principal's home had to be relocated after nearly washing out to sea during a fall storm in 2005.

Every year, villagers attempt to reinforce the seawall. They throw sandbags and weighted blocks into the breach, only to watch the ocean wash them away. And their efforts have only slowed the inevitable. It's just a matter of time before the entire island must be abandoned.

Where will they go? Depending on their choice, it will cost somewhere between $150 to $250 million to relocate the village. And so far, no one has stepped up to foot the bill.

As Climate Changes, Traditions Fail

Nearly 80 percent of the Inupiaq diet comes from animals they catch. Traditional instructions, handed down from generation to generation, inform them when the ice is thick enough to hunt whale and bear, when the caribou arrive, and when the salmon swim upstream to spawn.

For centuries, the Inupiaq stored their food in underground storage caves called *siglauqs*. Buried in the frozen ground, these caves acted as freezers. Meat obtained in the spring was carefully wrapped in seal blubber and stored in the caves for winter consumption.

Kivalina has two of these caves about a mile east of town on the mainland, far from the ocean. Last year, the people were alarmed to discover that one of the caves had been flooded with more than five feet of water and their community's food was entirely spoiled. The permafrost was no more, and the ground had melted, flooding the caves.

Soon, water will almost certainly flood the second storage cave. Once the second cave is gone, the villagers have no idea how they will store and age the meats that form an essential part of their diet. There aren't a lot of freezers big enough to store whole seals.

Their hunting and storage methods, developed over centuries, enable the Inupiaq to adapt to what many of us would consider a hostile and forbidding environment. But now their traditional methods are failing them. Hunters are increasingly at risk on ice that now thins earlier in the year. Caribou populations are affected by warmer winter temperatures, which can cause a shell of ice to form over the snow. This prevents the caribou from feeding on the grass below. In some cases, individual herds have been decimated within a single winter.

Whale and seal, staples of the Inuit diet, have been shifting their ranges. Many experts believe this is due to warming ocean temperatures and changes in the length of the ice-free season. And polar bears, those enduring symbols of the frozen Arctic, have been listed as threatened under the endangered species list. The Arctic ice—where polar bears live, hunt, and even den—has been melting so fast that scientists estimate the entire Arctic summer could be ice-free within just a few years. Some wonder whether polar bears will even live to see the next century.

The Changing Arctic

On their own, the changes at Kivalina might be passed off as a localized phenomenon—tragic for the Inupiaq people, but not indicative of global trends. Unfortunately, this is not the case. Effects like those seen in Kivalina are widespread.

Many towns and villages across Alaska are experiencing the same types of changes as Kivalina. Protective shore ice is forming later in the year and breaking up earlier. Increasingly fierce storms are pounding the unprotected coasts, eroding the coastline, and endangering its inhabitants. Previously solid, frozen ground is cracking and melting, creating enormous fissures and sinkholes in the ground, some of these hundreds of feet across. This leads to "drunken forests," with trees leaning every which way; large fissures and cracks in roads, sidewalks, and runways; and houses that have split down the middle or even fallen over sideways as a large hole opened up unexpectedly beside them. Travel over frozen ground in the Arctic has been cut from seven to four months per year, isolating many communities. Long-standing patterns of how land and marine animals come and go with the seasons are changing.

All these changes have one thing in common: they're all linked to warming temperatures—warming that is being seen, not just in Alaska, but around the world.

2

OUR CHANGING PLANET

"Climate change is for real."

—Bishop Desmond Tutu

Temperatures are rising. Seasonal patterns are shifting. Spring is coming earlier in the year. Summers are getting hotter. Mountain glaciers are melting. Sea levels are rising. Before our very eyes, within the space of one short generation, our world is undergoing a radical transformation.

In the United States, warmer temperatures have shifted the geographical ranges of many of our native plant and animal species, altering the timing of flowering and breeding. Ice on lakes and rivers is forming later in the year, and melting earlier. In the dry Western states, more winter precipitation is falling as rain, and less as snow. The snow they do get is now melting three weeks earlier in the spring. Warmer temperatures and earlier springs are increasing wildfire activity.

In Europe, increasingly warmer temperatures have melted two-thirds of the volume of Alpine glaciers. The melting began in the 1900s and has accelerated in the last few decades. And warmer temperatures have brought more frequent heat waves, including the killer heat wave of 2003, responsible for more than seventy thousand deaths in France and surrounding countries.

How unusual are these events? And how can we be sure they're part of a global pattern? What kinds of records can actually tell us if global climate change is truly happening? These are just some of the questions we're going to address head-on. So, if you're ready, let's jump right in.

Global Temperatures: 150 Years of Records

The most reliable indicators of climate change are temperature records. And nothing measures temperature better than the simple thermometer.

During the 1700s and 1800s, weather stations with thermometers and rain gauges started cropping up all over Europe, North America, Asia, Australia, and Africa. By the mid-1800s, enough weather stations were situated around the world to begin to calculate global average temperature.

Weather stations around the world are now regulated by the World Meteorological Organization. This organization makes sure temperatures are measured at the same time of day, using the same instruments, at a fixed height above the ground, by trained observers.

To accurately calculate Earth's average temperature, scientists take into account any abnormalities at weather stations that would cause jumps or false trends in the record. They also ensure that a region with only one station covering a very large area is represented as equally in the global average as another region with a much higher concentration of stations. Scientists then average together all the information they have to get a global picture of what Earth's temperature has looked like each year from 1850 until now (see Figure 2).

1850 to Present

From 1850 to about 1910, Earth's temperature remained fairly constant. Then from 1910 to 1940, temperatures rose. After 1940, they flattened out for a few decades until about 1970. Scientists believe this temporary damper on warming was at least partially caused by the massive "dust blanket" humans produced during that time, combined with natural variations in the climate system. Since 1970, temperatures have been rising steadily.

From these observations, we see a global temperature increase of 1.3°F since 1900. Out of nearly 160 years of records, the ten warmest years have all occurred since 1997. The warmest year ever was 1998, followed by 2005 and 2003.

Average temperatures across the United States have risen even faster than the global average, more than 2°F since 1950. In the western and northern United States, temperatures have risen on average 70 percent faster than the global average; in some parts of Alaska, by as much as 4°F.

The warmest year on record in the United States was 1998, followed by 2006. Although 2007 was only the tenth warmest year on record for the United States, maximum temperature records were broken that year at 263 different weather stations.

The year 2008 seemed a bit cold; and it's true that temperatures in 2008 were the lowest they've been since 2000. Even still, temperatures in the United States were well above average in 2008. And if we look at the global record, we can see that 2008 was actually the tenth warmest year on record. A few decades ago, 2008 would have felt like an abnormally warm year. What's happened is that we've grown so accustomed to unusually warm temperatures that what used to be normal now feels cold. The truth is that our temperatures today are very unusual in the context of the historical record. Just how unusual they are can be seen more clearly when we look at an even longer record of temperature.

Central England Temperature: A 350-Year History

The oldest collection of thermometer-based temperature records we have are preserved in the annals of the Central England Temperature. Dating back to 1659, these records show 350 years of hot days and cold ones, sweltering highs and frigid lows, captured faithfully each month in a triangular region between Bristol, Lancashire, and London.

The Central England Temperature record, illustrated in Figure 3 in the color insert, gives us a bird's-eye view of temperature change in England for nearly four centuries. It shows us, of course, that temperatures can change dramatically from one year to the next. But climate change is about whether any pattern can be seen over thirty years or more.

Do we see any long-term trend in this lengthy and meticulous record? Yes, temperatures in recent decades have indeed been unusually warm in comparison to the long-term average in Central England. And this warming is also consistent with what we see at the global level.

The hottest year in the Central England record was 2006, with 1990 and 1999 in a dead heat—pun intended—for second place. The record for the coldest year has not been broken since 1740!

No Cooling in Sight

Despite the evidence for a warming trend from the global record, some still claim that global warming has slowed down, or that "it's not much of a problem anymore," or even "it's stopped." Talk of global *cooling*, first heard in the 1970s, has recently resurfaced.

It's true that, if the sun alone were controlling our climate, there would be reason to suspect that we're headed for a new ice age—eventually. This was the logic proposed in a handful of scientific journal articles and one *Newsweek* story in the 1970s.

But today, we know the sun is not the only factor. As we'll discuss later, the idea that greenhouse gases are driving climate has been around for more than 150 years. And this theory has been the subject of tens of thousands of scientific journal articles.

Even still, the notion of global cooling has recently resurfaced, and Figure 4 in the center insert helps explain why. This graph zooms in on global temperatures over the last fifty years. The red line shows how temperatures have been rising from 1960 to 2008, while the blue line shows how you can use this same record to support an argument that the world actually cooled from 1998 to 2008. Some carefully select these two data points to argue that climate change isn't occurring. Or they even claim that the world is cooling.

It's true that the blue line from 1998 to 2008 slopes downward. At first glance, one might think this suggests that global warming is slowing down. But climate change is about what is happening across decades and centuries. It's certainly not about the difference between two specifically selected years.

The true change in global temperature—an undeniable warming—is seen by drawing a line across multiple decades. Here, we see 1960 to 2008, for example. And, in Figure 2, we see global temperatures from 1850 to 2008. These longer-term graphs accurately depict the warming trend we are experiencing, and illustrate the problem with selecting two individual years that are a decade apart, connecting the dots, and then arguing for global cooling.

Reliable Temperature Records

Some will protest, "The temperature record is contaminated by the urban heat island effect. Cities are hotter than the rural areas, and most thermometers are in the cities!" This is an important argument to address, because the urban heat island effect is real. But the temperature record used by climate scientists already accounts for the urban heat island effect. It is fully reliable.

The urban heat island phenomenon was first documented by British chemist and amateur meteorologist Luke Howard. In 1820, he showed that temperatures in the city of London were usually several degrees warmer than in the surrounding countryside.

Howard's observation was the first solid scientific evidence for the urban heat island effect. This effect occurs when the dark surfaces of roads and buildings heat up faster than the green countryside. The dark surfaces also retain the heat longer at night. Together, this means that temperatures in urban areas can be up to 10°F hotter than outside the city.

So what does this have to do with the temperature record from thermometers? Originally, most weather stations were located in cities so that observers wouldn't have to travel too far to take their measurements. Over time, rooftops and pavement spread far and wide, increasing the strength of the urban heat island effect and artificially raising local temperatures.

You can see the problem. If temperature measurements have not accounted for an increase in the urban heat island effect over time, what we have measured might simply be that increase. How can we tell if there has been any real change in temperature?

The Urban Heat Island Effect

How well do scientists account for the urban heat island effect when they calculate global average temperature? A battery of tests suggests that, actually, scientists have done a very good job of removing the urban heat island effect from the global record.

The first and simplest way to see this is by looking at a map that shows us where people live. In the center insert, Figure 5 shows a picture of Earth at night, taken from space. What you're looking at here are the lights from roads, highways, and buildings. These are the areas where people actually live. And these areas are where the urban heat island effect is strongest.

Now, let's compare this to a map showing where temperatures have warmed the most. If most of the warming were simply because of urbanization, we would expect to see "hot spots" over the big, lighted, urban areas: Japan, western Europe, and eastern United

States. Instead, what we actually see is that the largest warming is happening over mostly uninhabited areas: Alaska, the Northwest Territories, and Siberia. And a lot of warming is happening over ocean-covered areas as well. So, contrary to arguments based on the urban heat island effect, global warming is not happening *only* in major urban areas. It's happening in a major way in *un*inhabited regions of our planet as well.

We get the same results no matter how we sort and examine the global data. We can remove stations that stopped recording temperature in recent decades. We can remove stations that just opened recently. We can even remove all of the urban stations from the record. And we *still* end up with the same result—a steady increase in temperature over the last century.

There is no evidence that our current warming trend can be explained by the urban heat island effect. Something strange is definitely happening on our planet.

3

INDICATORS OF CHANGE

"Current global temperatures are warmer than they have ever been during at least the past five centuries, probably even for more than a millennium."
—The Intergovernmental Panel on Climate Change

In comparison to the last few centuries, for a few decades now Earth's temperature has been extraordinarily warm. But are conditions today still all that unusual if we go even further back in time?

Climate records from the past help put our current situation in context of what we've experienced before. The further back we go, the more we see how humans have always faced temperature increases and decreases, major droughts and extended rains, hurricanes and monsoons. Sometimes we have successfully dealt with these changes. At other times these events have triggered the collapse of entire civilizations.

But even the oldest thermometer records only go back to 1659. So how do we know what temperatures were like before that?

Natural Thermometers

For centuries, people around the world have been noting seasonal markers of change. These records of "natural thermometers" include detailed accounts of harvest dates, flowering times, when the river ice broke up, and whether a particular year was abnormally hot or dry, cold or wet. Records go back more than a thousand years at some locations in China, Japan, Europe, and North America.

These historical records of "natural" thermometers aren't as easy to interpret as actual temperature measurements. But they do give a good idea of relative changes over time. These changes help us understand just how unusual the last few decades have been in the history of human civilization.

For example, old paintings show glacier-covered valleys that are now ice-free. Lakes and rivers are freezing later or even less frequently than in past centuries. Grape harvests are ripening more quickly. All of these help indicate whether today is warmer than it used to be one hundred or even one thousand years ago in the same location.

Japan's Cherry Trees

Japanese cherry blossom festivals, known as *hanami* ("flower-viewing"), typically last about one week. During this time, Japanese people take time off to travel and observe the splendor of the blooming trees. The city of Kyoto has been the most popular destination for more than one thousand years.

The dates of these festivals have been meticulously recorded in journals and diaries over time. They've also been captured in poems, songs, and paintings. Painstaking research has enabled Japanese scientists to compile an exact record of festival dates extending back more than a thousand years. And here's what they've found.

The first two centuries or so show relatively early flowering dates, suggesting relatively warm temperatures during the Middle Ages. Later flowering dates were recorded from 1600 to 1800, indicating cooler temperatures. But since 1800, the dates have become steadily earlier. This is consistent with the warming that we are witnessing all over the globe.

By the 1980s and early 1990s, flowering times in Kyoto were earlier than any time in the last thousand years, and this trend continues today. This long-term record is just one example of how unusual today's conditions are relative to any recent history.

The same type of cherry trees were given to the United States as a gift by Japan in 1912. They were planted around the Jefferson Memorial in Washington, D.C. The flowering of these cherry trees has now also become a major tourist draw in springtime. And our record of flowering dates, going back nearly one hundred years, also indicate that these trees are flowering nearly a week earlier on average than they used to.

Ancient Trees and Coral Reefs

There are other "natural thermometers" that have nothing to do with humans recording facts and figures. Climate records are preserved in trees and coral reefs, for example, and in stalactites and stalagmites. These capture hundreds of years of history as they grow.

The rings inside a tree, for example, tell us what temperature and rainfall were like for each year of the tree's life. Starting at the outer edge of the tree, you step back in time as you count the rings toward the center. In Figure 6, Andrew points to the rings of a thousand-year-old redwood tree in California. White lines mark the dates of important events such as Columbus discovering America.

For some long-lived trees, such as bristlecone pines in the United States and river oaks in Germany, complete records extend back thousands of years. The longest record in the world, using a single tree species, comes from the White Mountains in the California desert. From both living trees and fallen logs, researchers have assembled a temperature record extending back nine thousand years. Using these natural records, we learn a great deal about how climate has changed.

Coral reefs also preserve records of how ocean temperatures have changed over time. As coral grows, it absorbs one of two kinds of oxygen, standard or deuterium, from the seawater. Where the coral holds more standard oxygen, it tells us that the ocean water was cooler. Where the coral holds more deuterium, it tells us that the ocean water was warmer. The age of coral is discovered by counting its layers, from top to bottom. One layer of coral roughly represents one year of time. From changes in the oxygen ratios (standard versus deuterium), scientists can infer changes in temperature over the life span of the coral.

Both tree and coral records help us determine if the recent warming we're witnessing is unusual. And both the trees and the coral are shouting a resounding "Yes!" Today's warming trend is unlike any they've experienced before.

The Hockey Stick: Unusual Warming

When scientists combine recent records from actual thermometers with more extensive records from these "natural thermometers," they can see further into the past.

Natural thermometer records have been assembled in enough locations around the world to extend average global temperature records back nearly to New Testament times (AD 200). And records for individual locations can go back much further than that.

When we graph temperature over the last two thousand years (as shown in Figure 7), we end up with a hockey-stick-shaped line. The cooler, flat line endures for almost two thousand years. This is the handle of the hockey stick. Then, there's a sharp curve upward over the last two hundred years—the blade of the hockey stick. This depicts our recent warming trend.

As far back as we can go with both actual thermometers and "natural thermometers," the conclusions are the same:

- Our globe *is* now warming.
- The current warming appears to be unique in our history.
- The warming coincides with the dawn of the Industrial Age.

Despite numerous challenges by skeptics, the "hockey stick" record of historical temperature has been repeatedly shown to be valid and reliable. It tells us that the warming we are seeing today is unprecedented over at least the last two thousand years.

Medieval Warming and the Little Ice Age

Although the warming we are seeing today is far greater than anything in the "natural thermometer" record, that doesn't mean that we haven't experienced important climate changes in the past. As you can see from Figure 7, from about the tenth to the fourteenth centuries, temperatures in western Europe, Greenland, and eastern Canada were warmer than average. During this time, known as the Medieval Warm Period, the Vikings colonized Greenland and Newfoundland.

After this warm period, the Northern Hemisphere experienced cooler temperatures that lasted from about 1650 to the mid-1800s. This is often referred to as the Little Ice Age. During much of that period, Greenland was cut off by ice, and crop failure and famine were commonplace. Farmers were hard-pressed to adapt to a much shorter growing season and more frequent cold weather. This cooler period lasted nearly two hundred years until our current warming trend took over.

Despite the overwhelming evidence that this "hockey stick" temperature diagram is accurate, some continue to claim that it used to be much warmer in medieval times than today. They then conclude that we don't need to worry about the current warming since it's nothing out of the ordinary.

This claim ignores the fundamental differences between the medieval warming and today's. First, the former was *regional* in nature. Medieval warming was restricted to the North Atlantic where most of Western civilization was living at the time. This regional warming is thought to be tied to changes in Atlantic currents that carried heat from the tropics toward Newfoundland, and then on into Europe. But temperatures in the Pacific were slightly colder than usual during this same time period. And global temperature averages show no overall warming. Hence, claims of a medieval warming are only relevant to *one particular region* of the globe.

Second, the medieval warming did not result in warmer temperatures than we're witnessing today. And lastly, the medieval warming was the result of natural causes, not human causes.

Today's warming is different. The entire globe is warming, from Antarctica to the Arctic Ocean. This warming is already greater than anything we've seen in the past, going back one, two, even five thousand years. And it's also *un*natural. For the first time in history, we humans are altering Earth's climate.

4

DECISIONS AND CONSEQUENCES

"Though the claims of science are neither infallible nor unanimous, they are substantial and cannot be dismissed out of hand on either scientific or theological grounds."
—*A Southern Baptist Declaration on the Environment and Climate Change* (2008)

The evidence for climate change is in. When we separate fact from persuasive fiction, the strong, clear signals from nature itself are even more evident. Our planet is experiencing an unusual warming.

So let's pause to consider this warming in light of our identity, as children of the creative God who spoke into existence this unique planet He has given us.

Is concurring that global warming is indeed happening somehow contrary to our beliefs as Christians? Not at all. In fact, the opposite is true. From Genesis onward, we learn how God specifically designed the world to be one of constant change: from day to night, summer to winter, and rainy season to dry. There is certainly nothing inherently "Christian" about clinging to a belief that global temperatures are not increasing, especially in light of the physical evidence.

We Christians should actually be doing the opposite. Peter instructs us to "be of sound judgment" (1 Pet. 4:7 NASB), and Paul tells us to think on truth, not error (Phil. 4:8 NIV). Sure, God created the ostrich, but not as an example of what we should do when we're confronted with an issue that we prefer would just go away!

Facing the Truth

No one in the Bible ever had to face the decision of what to believe and do about global warming. But many of them were confronted with other unpleasant truths. Of the heroes of faith listed in Hebrews 11, most were people who stood up, looked an unpleasant truth in the eye, and then set about doing what they felt was necessary. They did not sit around and think of every possible reason in the world why that truth might instead be false.

That's not to say there weren't some who wanted to be very sure before they did anything. Remember the story of Gideon in Judges 6, when he was told he had to save Israel from the Midianites? First, he wanted the fleece to be wet and the ground to remain dry, and so it was. "But what if it happened by accident?" Gideon asked. So then he asked for the fleece to remain dry, but the ground to be wet. And that happened too!

Gideon was a pragmatic man; he'd checked as much as he could. So the next we see of him, he has gathered the people of Israel and is on his way to attack the Midianite camp, just as the angel had originally told him to do.

The First Fleece: Consequences of Inaction

In the same way, climate change merits a good, hard look and a few well-laid fleeces before we make any final decisions. Because, with either position on climate change, we are locking ourselves into a decision with significant consequences. This is especially true if we decide that human-induced climate change is a myth and then it turns out to be an all-too-present reality.

Say, for example, we decide there is nothing to this climate change thing. It's not really happening. Or, temperatures may have gone up temporarily, but soon they'll go right back down again. This is just a natural cycle, we conclude, and there's nothing we can do about it. Then we keep on living the way we have been for the past century, assuming that nothing is changing. We plan for tomorrow's conditions to be the same as those we've known over the past century.

What happens if we end up being *wrong*?

It is true that the first degree or two of warming may bring modest benefits to northern countries—warmer winters, less snow and ice, longer growing seasons. However, poorer nations will still suffer harmful and costly consequences even from small temperature increases. In addition, any early benefits we enjoy in the North from slightly warmer temperatures will soon disappear, to be followed by harmful conditions. And as our actions continue to affect Earth's climate more and more, the likelihood of disastrous impacts increases.

By the time our mistaken position on global warming becomes obvious to us, we would be so far down the climate change road that:

- The massive ice sheets of Greenland and west Antarctica could be destabilized, guaranteeing the eventual loss of many of the world's largest cities to a rise in sea level of forty feet or more over coming centuries.
- A substantial fraction of the world's species could be doomed to extinction.
- The Amazon rain forest, already threatened by widespread deforestation, would be dying off at a massive scale.
- Extreme drought would threaten as much as a third of the world, taking over many agricultural areas and leading to mass migrations of "environmental refugees."
- Our children and grandchildren could be living in a world increasingly characterized by severe droughts, massive heat waves, and worldwide conflicts due to food and water shortages.

As you can imagine, the economic costs of these changes are

estimated to be enormous. It is impossible to put a global price tag on the cost of inaction. But individual studies estimate net costs in the billions of dollars for individual states alone. Globally, costs on the order of 20 percent or more of the world's economy are estimated under these circumstances, an order of magnitude higher than the costs of reducing emissions and avoiding the worst of these consequences.

Of course, we cannot be certain that *all* of this would happen as a result of our inaction. But scientists warn us that if this current warming trend *is* human-induced, then it's likely that our world will turn into a very different place than what we're used to if we don't start changing our habits now. There is a serious risk to deciding that climate change is not real.

Intuitively, we know all about risk. That's the reason we buy insurance. We spend hundreds, even thousands, of dollars every year to avoid the unpleasant nature of risk. We are perfectly willing to pay a small amount up front in order to ensure that we won't face a much larger cost down the road.

So if we were to make a decision about climate change following the same approach we take with our auto or home insurance, we'd probably be doing something about climate change right now. And we'd probably invest in that security even if we thought there wasn't much chance that something bad would actually happen. The actual risk involved with global climate change is higher than many of us are normally willing to accept in our personal lives.

There are many other good reasons for taking positive action against global warming, in addition to reducing our effect on Earth's climate. By reducing our reliance on coal, gas, and oil and looking to clean, renewable sources for our energy, we would:

- clean up our air and water.
- reduce our dependence on foreign oil.

- invest in our own economy and our people.
- preserve our natural resources for future generations.

Doesn't that just make good sense?

The Second Fleece: The Benefits of Action

Now what if humans really are the cause of this warming trend? If so, then we need to be honest. Fixing the climate change problem will not be easy. It will eventually require nothing less than the transformation of our society.

Unfortunately, our contributions to the increase in heat-trapping gases are woven throughout the fabric of our lives. Disentangling those strands and replacing them with healthy, viable alternatives will require a lot of careful thought, diligent work, and smart investment.

Accomplishing this ambitious goal will not be easy, but it is possible. And it carries with it all the side benefits we listed before. It may be more affordable than we currently imagine, especially when compared with the cost of inaction. But it will still cost *something*, and that something will be quite large compared to *nothing*.

Before we take any radical action, we need to be certain that our current warming is indeed a result of human activity. In particular, it behooves us to take a careful look at other possible causes of temperature change. Aren't there a lot of other reasons why Earth's temperature has changed in the past: volcanoes, natural cycles, the sun? What's so different about today's changes?

Our Marked Fleece: Undeniable Evidence of Change

Wouldn't it be ideal if we, like Gideon, had a fleece to lay out today? Maybe in the morning it would read "Global warming is real!" in big green letters if God wanted us to be convinced of climate change.

But God has given us some help here. We have all kinds of ways to observe Earth. And these observations have already given us some very solid answers regarding what is happening, and why it's happening—sort of like a modern, high-tech fleece.

Today, the consensus of climate scientists worldwide is that the majority of the warming we have seen over the last fifty years is a result of human emissions of heat-trapping gases. These gases have been released into the air as we burn coal, oil, and gas to heat and cool our homes, drive our cars, and power our factories. These gases are trapping heat given off by the earth that would otherwise escape to space.

The fleece has been marked. Our actions are inadvertently affecting the world's climate. And unfortunately, it's not a positive effect that we are having.

We never intended to bring about all these effects back in the 1700s when we first learned to use coal to run steam engines. But unless we respond now, having already seen what's happening in more sensitive places like Kivalina, we may soon face similar dangers in our own backyard.

part two

causes

5

GOD'S GIFT: THE EARTH

"For all its epic scale, the God-drawn balance of climate is remarkably fragile."

—Peter Illyn, Restoring Eden

To better understand what is happening with climate change, we first need to take a step back to admire the brilliant design and positioning of our planet. When we do this, the first thing we notice is how very different Planet Earth is from all the others in our solar system. Earth is perfectly suited for life.

Mercury is a cratered ball of yellowish-gray rock. Venus is cloaked by swirling white and yellow clouds of carbon dioxide, and choking heat. The surface of Mars is rocky and red, dominated by volcanic channels. And the outer planets alternate between giant gaseous spheres and lifeless balls of rock.

In contrast, Earth's wide blue oceans and fertile green lands support fantastically diverse life-forms, from the glowing fish that inhabit undersea trenches to the elephants that roam the African plains. And temperatures rarely go beyond the limits of what its inhabitants can tolerate.

A Natural Balance

The reason temperatures here on Earth are so stable is because we have an *atmosphere*, a thin shell of gases that wraps around the planet. The sun's rays heat Earth. But heat-trapping greenhouse gases in the atmosphere act just like a blanket on a cold night. They trap much of Earth's heat that would otherwise escape to space.

This perfectly designed balance keeps Earth from heating up too much during the day. It also prevents Earth from cooling down too much at night. Our natural blanket, the atmosphere, maintains the average temperature of Earth at a very pleasant 55°F instead of the frigid 0°F that it would be otherwise.

As the sun's energy enters the atmosphere, about one-third of it gets reflected back to space. Two-thirds is absorbed by the earth's surface. The earth's surface then heats up and gives off heat in order to "cool off" like when we sweat. But we need that heat to keep our planet from turning into a frozen ball of ice. And that's where greenhouse gases come in.

The most important gas that helps maintain this much-needed temperature balance on Earth is water vapor. Water vapor absorbs so completely that, for centuries, scientists thought water vapor was doing *all* the work of keeping Earth's temperatures in check. Not until this last century did they discover that there are other greenhouse gases that also absorb the earth's heat. These other gases, including carbon dioxide, methane, and nitrous oxide, account for 15–35 percent of the natural heat-trapping greenhouse effect.

This natural greenhouse effect is what makes our planet livable and unique among all the other planets. The natural greenhouse effect is a beautiful example of the care God has taken in creating a planet so perfectly suited for life. Earth has been carefully balanced to provide a comfortable home for the human race.

Gases of Life

Natural greenhouse gases are critical to life on Earth. Their fragile balance must be maintained so the earth and its inhabitants can thrive.

Today, carbon dioxide, methane, and other greenhouse gases are often referred to as *pollutants*. But pollutants remind us of sickly yellow fogs that hover over our cities, signaling us not to breathe too deeply. In contrast, greenhouse gases are colorless. You can't see them, and you can't smell them. If you were to walk into a room entirely filled with carbon dioxide, it would look and smell normal to you; although you wouldn't survive for long!

We depend on carbon for our existence. Every breath we take, we breathe in oxygen. It combines with carbon in our bodies, and we exhale carbon dioxide. Our very breath contributes to the balance the earth maintains for us.

Plants need carbon dioxide to grow. During the day, they absorb carbon dioxide from the atmosphere, using it as the building blocks for their leaves and roots. They breathe out as we do, releasing excess carbon dioxide back into the atmosphere.

All of this—human breath, plant activity, and even cycling levels of water vapor, carbon dioxide, and other gases in the atmosphere—are accounted for in the natural greenhouse effect. But scientists are not concerned about the *natural* greenhouse effect. What they are worried about is the *enhanced* greenhouse effect that we're seeing today. This enhanced effect is the result of our production and release of increasingly large, unnatural amounts of carbon dioxide, nitrous oxide, and methane into the atmosphere.

Since the Industrial Revolution, we've been pumping out more and more greenhouse gases. Figure 9 shows where these gases have been coming from—our industry, agriculture, electricity generation, and transportation. This production has raised the natural levels, enhancing the natural greenhouse effect beyond what was intended. Just as adding an extra blanket on an already-warm night will make you sweat, we are adding an extra "blanket" to the earth in the form of these heat-trapping gases. And the earth is beginning to overheat.

Our planet cannot cope with this abnormal, unnatural increase of greenhouse gases. We already had just the right amount of carbon dioxide and other greenhouse gases in our atmosphere. By adding to that amount, we are tipping the natural balance that God created for us. And we're just beginning to see the consequences of that unbalance: Earth's rising temperature.

Tipping the Balance: Carbon Dioxide Out of Control

The atmosphere, plant life, and the earth itself are involved in a constant cycle of carbon dioxide exchange, release and renewal. Every year the ocean releases more than 90 billion tons of carbon dioxide into the atmosphere. Plants and trees produce about 120 billion tons. Together, natural sources produce more than 200 billion tons of carbon dioxide per year.

Today, human emissions total over 8 billion tons per year. At first glance, it would appear that any human emissions of carbon dioxide are insignificant when compared with the earth's natural output. But we must remember to see things in terms of balance. Although plants, trees, and oceans are indeed pumping enormous amounts of carbon dioxide into the atmosphere, they also take equal amounts out. On average, oceans, trees, and plants absorb as much or more carbon dioxide than they produce. In contrast, our production of carbon dioxide has skyrocketed in the past two hundred years.

Through our activities, we don't *remove* any carbon dioxide from the atmosphere. Instead, we only add carbon dioxide, methane, and other gases to the air. And most of what we put into the atmosphere stays there. It builds up, thickening that protective blanket and warming the earth more and more. So even 5 percent of what trees, plants, and oceans produce is enough to throw the earth's delicate balance entirely out of whack.

No matter what some may claim, the impact we are having is *serious*. Five percent per year might not sound like much, but since the Industrial Revolution, cumulative emissions have added up to more than 200 billion tons. Thirty percent of that total, some 60 billion tons, has come from the United States alone (see Figure 8, a map of carbon dioxide emissions by country). And much of that is still sitting in the atmosphere today.

Figuring in the Flatulence

But there's more to global warming than just carbon dioxide. Methane, although produced in much smaller amounts than carbon dioxide, absorbs twenty-five times as much heat. So one methane unit released into the atmosphere is like releasing twenty-five carbon units. And we're producing more and more methane every day.

The main source of methane is the decay of organic matter. Plant decomposition, animal waste, human waste, and underwater bacteria in shallow wetlands and rice fields produce more than three-quarters of the world's methane. Mining for coal and natural gas also releases deep pockets of methane buried far below Earth's crust.

You may have heard that cows, goats, sheep, and buffalo also produce a lot of methane gas. These cud-chewing mammals have multiple stomachs for digesting food. During digestion, bacteria in their stomachs produce methane.

How does this methane in the stomach eventually escape from the cow? About 90 percent of it is released via cow burps. And you can probably guess how the other 10 percent gets released.

You may also wonder how a harmless cow could be a significant contributor of methane gas, especially given that large numbers of wild animals once roamed the earth and are now gone. Surely they must have released methane too! So how can animal methane production be worse today?

The difference lies in the fact that, in comparison to the number of wild animals that used to roam the Great Plains, for example, we now raise an even greater number of cud-chewing, methane-emitting animals for food. And their methane production far outweighs any previous animal contributions. On top of this, human society now produces vast amounts of trash that decays, producing even more methane than ever before.

The Latest News

We have seen how increasing levels of carbon dioxide and methane are already causing problems for Earth.

Since 2000, however, global emissions have been increasing faster than even the highest emissions scenario that scientists use to make projections about the next century. Levels of carbon dioxide in the atmosphere have responded, rising 35 percent faster than expected. This is not just because of our accelerating emissions. It's also because oceans, trees, and plants may be starting to tell us, "We've had enough!" As we add more heat-trapping gases to the atmosphere, the ocean's ability to absorb these gases slows. Therefore, the more emissions we produce, the more we see those gases *remaining* in the atmosphere.

It's true that for a few years after the turn of the century, natural emissions of methane slowed down for a bit. Dry conditions cut down on methane production from natural sources such as northern wetlands and bogs. But now natural emissions are back to normal. And the level of methane in the atmosphere is increasing once again.

Increases in production of carbon dioxide, methane, and other heat-trapping gases enhance the natural greenhouse effect.

But how can we really be sure it's these gases that are causing climate change? Aren't there a lot of *other* natural factors that affect Earth's temperature?

6

THE NATURAL SUSPECTS

"The day is yours, and yours also the night;
   you established the sun and moon.
It was you who set all the boundaries of the earth;
   you made both summer and winter."
—Psalm 74:16–17 (TNIV)

But there's no proof that we are causing the warming! After all, we see lots of changes in *weather*: cold days and hot spells, torrential rain and droughts. And we have nothing to do with those! Heck, we can't even predict most of these events. They're due to natural causes—the sun, natural cycles, or even volcanoes. So why should we believe that climate is any different?

You have likely heard an argument like this before, on the radio, online, or even from your favorite television news program. But this book is not about short, slick arguments that can be presented in thirty-second sound bites. It's about taking a long, hard look at the evidence and making up our own minds, based on what God's other "book"—the natural world—tells us.

So the first thing we need to do is investigate those "usual suspects" and see what they've been up to lately. Do they have a solid alibi? Or should we simply pin the blame on them and go on with our lives as usual?

Suspect #1: The Sun

The sun is the first place to look if we're searching for an explanation for changes in Earth's temperature.

We already know that it's the orbit of the earth around the sun that causes our seasons to change from summer to winter, and back to summer again, every year.

Astronomers also tell us that the amount of energy we receive from the sun varies over an eleven-year cycle, by about one tenth of a percent. You can see this cycle in Figure 10. The purple line shows the changes in the amount of energy we receive from the sun. At the top of the cycle, we get more energy from the sun. At the bottom, we get a bit less.

Sometimes solar activity can temporarily shut down for decades at a time. This was the situation from about 1645 to 1715. This period also coincided with the coldest part of the Little Ice Age over Europe that we talked about earlier.

And over thousands and thousands of years, Earth's orbit undergoes slow, predictable changes in shape. The pathway that the earth follows around the sun becomes first more circular, and then more oval. The earth tilts more toward the sun, and then away from it. Together, these changes affect the amount of solar energy that Earth receives, as well as the time and place that energy is received.

These long-term, cyclical changes in the energy that the earth receives from the sun are the reason for the largest natural cycles the earth experiences. So it's entirely logical, when we see unusual change in global temperature, to look first to the sun as our prime suspect. But when we dig deeper, we encounter solid evidence that doesn't support our allegations.

That's because, for the last few decades, the sun has a perfect alibi.

As we've seen, many major changes in Earth's temperature in the past have been driven by changes in the sun's output. So let's take a look at what the sun has been doing lately. Can solar activity explain the unusual warming over the last century?

Figure 10 compares energy from the sun to the observed change in Earth's temperature. For the first part of the last century—up until about the mid-seventies—both temperature and energy from the sun were increasing. So it is very likely that the sun had a positive effect on temperature during that time.

But, for the last three decades, Earth's temperature has been increasing even more rapidly than before. And this has happened at the exact same time that solar energy has been holding constant or even going down.

Yes, that's right. Solar activity has been going down since the late 1980s as global temperatures continued to rise. If our temperature were being primarily controlled by the sun right now, then over the last few decades we should actually have seen temperatures *cooling*, not warming.

So if the natural-cycles argument is going to hold up in court, we're going to have to put another prime suspect on the witness stand. Let's try the earth's oceans and the atmosphere itself, to see if they can be guilty as charged.

Suspect #2: Natural Cycles

The most well-known natural cycle is El Niño, which means "the little boy" in Spanish. Named after the baby Jesus, El Niño was first identified as a pattern of warm ocean waters off the coast of Peru that tended to occur around Christmas.

Today, we know that El Niño extends as far west as Australia, changing wind, temperature, and rainfall patterns around the world. An El Niño year such as 1998 tends to be warmer than usual. In contrast, a La Niña year such as 2008 (where the ocean waters are cooler than normal) tends to produce cooler-than-average global temperatures.

El Niño events bring life-giving rain to some regions and severe droughts to others. In the dry, arid plains of west Texas, for example, a wet El Niño winter means that farmers can expect a break from the continuous irrigation usually needed to water the cotton crop that supports the region's economy.

It's not all good news, though. The strongest El Niño winter in recent memory occurred during the winter of 1997–1998. World-wide, it caused an estimated $32–$96 billion in damages. Southern California was slammed by violent winter storms and heavy rainfall events that triggered landslides and swept away highways and houses. At the same time, an exceptional drought triggered fires that devastated large areas of tropical rain forests.

Natural cycles like El Niño are internal to the atmosphere-ocean system. There are many other cycles, some decades in length, that can affect *regional* temperatures, rainfall patterns, and even the amount of ice in the Arctic. But all of these cycles are exactly that—cycles. They affect certain parts of the world, but not all. They redistribute heat between the atmosphere and the ocean, but they don't create more overall heat.

Furthermore, scientists can measure exactly how these natural cycles have changed over the last hundred years or more. And adding up their effects produces no net change in temperature at all, let alone a change as unusual as what has been observed in recent decades. But there are other external natural factors that may cause some years to be colder or warmer, wetter or drier than others. We'll look at the most likely factor next.

Suspect #3: Volcanoes

Another argument you may hear is that volcanoes produce more carbon dioxide than humans. It logically follows that volcanoes have been around forever, and we obviously can't *prevent* them from erupting. Are volcanoes to blame for the current warming?

Volcanoes do produce carbon dioxide and other greenhouse gases. And these emissions *used to be* much larger than what humans produced—a very long time ago. Today, however, carbon dioxide production from volcanoes is miniscule compared to the human contribution. Rather, the main effect of volcanic eruptions is to *cool* the planet, not to warm it.

Major volcanic eruptions can shoot millions of tons of dust and ash far up into the atmosphere. These dust particles are so high that they can remain up there for several months and even years, circling the globe again and again. And the cooling effect of these dust clouds can be severe.

The eruption of Mount Tambora in Indonesia in 1815 was estimated to be the worst in the last twelve hundred years or more. The eruption was the reason why 1816 was known as the "year without a summer." Freezing summer temperatures, frosts, and even snowstorms destroyed crops across China, Europe, and eastern North America, causing the worst famine of the 1800s. Food shortages combined with flooding led to riots, and these events are estimated to have caused at least two hundred thousand deaths during that year.

Even today, we see that volcanoes have a cooling effect on the earth. Major eruptions such as Indonesia's Mount Agung in 1963, Mexico's El Chinchón in 1982, and the Philippines' Mount Pinatubo in 1992 had major—albeit temporary—cooling effects on temperatures worldwide. But today, we know when a volcano erupts and we can track its effects around the world. And the volcanic eruptions we've seen over the last century cannot be responsible for the sustained, global-scale warming we've been witnessing for more than a hundred years.

So if the sun, natural cycles, and volcanoes can't be blamed for what we see happening with our climate in recent decades, where should we look?

7

THE HUMAN FINGERPRINT

"The facts are conclusive—humankind's burning of fossil fuels has been a key contributor to climate change in the past 150 years. We believe that urgent action must be taken to cut our meddling in God's providential systems."
—Evangelical Youth Climate Initiative

We know that Earth's temperature is increasing. We have looked to the sun, to natural cycles, and to other components of the natural world to see if these can explain our present warming—and they cannot.

We do know that human emissions and atmospheric levels of greenhouse gases have been increasing over the last century. Chemistry 101 tells us that these gases trap heat. And so it is only logical to suspect that these gases may be holding heat inside our atmosphere that would otherwise escape to space.

So the next place to look is right here at home. Is there a logical chain of evidence to connect human production of heat-trapping gases to the changes we have seen taking place around the world? Can a "human fingerprint" be lifted from the evidence surrounding these recent changes? Are we indeed responsible?

The vast majority of scientists say *yes*. Today, scientists are virtually certain that most of the change observed over the last fifty years has our fingerprints all over it. And here is why.

The heat-trapping properties of greenhouse gases have never been in dispute. This can be easily verified in any chemistry laboratory with equipment that has been around for hundreds of years. We know what these gases do. The only questions we need to answer are:

- Have levels of these gases increased over the last century?
- Who or what is responsible for these increases?
- Are these increases enough to cause global warming?

Fossil Fuels and the Industrial Revolution

Since the Industrial Revolution, we've been using more and more coal, natural gas, and oil to power our houses, factories, and cars. Burning these "fossil" fuels combines carbon with oxygen to form carbon dioxide.

We can easily compare how much coal, gas, and oil we have used over the last 150 years to what has happened with carbon dioxide levels in the atmosphere. Figure 11 shows that comparison. And what we see is that changes in atmospheric levels of carbon dioxide, methane, and other greenhouse gases began in the late 1700s. This was precisely when we figured out how to burn massive amounts of coal, gas, and oil for energy.

Estimates of coal, oil, and gas that have been burned from then until now help us estimate what the corresponding carbon dioxide levels in the atmosphere should theoretically be. Atmospheric buildup is actually a bit less than what we'd expect from this calculation. This is because plants, trees, and the ocean have been helping us out. They've been increasing their uptake of carbon dioxide over that same time period. But it's not enough, and we can't count on that help to endure.

How can we tell if this increase is a big deal, though? We can do that by comparing today's levels to what has occurred in the past. Atmospheric measurements of atmospheric carbon dioxide and other greenhouse gas levels go back more than half a century, and ice-core records of carbon dioxide and methane extend back for millennia.

Ice core records are formed by snow falling, compacting the underlying snow into ice. Air trapped in the ice preserves a tiny part of atmosphere at the time the snow was converted to ice. Scientists travel to Antarctica and Greenland to drill long cores of ice, as shown in Figure 15. Just like tree rings and coral, scientists can begin at the top of today's ice and work their way backward in time. They measure the gas content of the ice bubbles as they go along to see how conditions have changed.

As far back as we can go in these records, we see that carbon dioxide has varied between 200 and, at most, 300 parts per million in the atmosphere. Methane has varied between 300 and a maximum of 700 parts per billion. Today, carbon dioxide stands at nearly 390 parts per million and methane at 1800 parts per billion. Today, both of these gases are at levels far beyond anything seen as part of natural cycles in the past.

So there is no question that atmospheric levels of greenhouse gases have increased dramatically since the Industrial Revolution. Their present-day levels are unusually high as compared to the historical record. And our industrialization has been inadvertently responsible for the majority of this change.

But how do we really know that it's the increase in gases that is causing our present warming?

A Virtual Earth: What Climate Models Tell Us

It would be easy to prove that the increase in greenhouse gases from industrialization caused our temperature change if we just had a second earth. We'd need one identical to our own, except with no people on it. Then we'd be able to observe what conditions were like on that second earth without any changes in greenhouse gas levels. We could then compare one planet to the other to verify the effects that people and industrialization were having on the planet.

But, of course, that's not possible.

Instead, scientists create a series of virtual earths, complex computer models of Earth's climate system. These models can be used to figure out what might be causing the unusual temperature increases we've seen. These models also help us determine what to expect in the future.

The very first climate models of the 1950s were originally intended as thought experiments. Scientists wondered if it were even possible to use the fundamental equations of physics to simulate our atmosphere and ocean. Early climate modelers were surprised when these simple models were able to reproduce many features of the known world, such as atmospheric circulation and ocean currents.

Climate models have come a long way since those days. Today, these sophisticated models are among the most time-intensive pieces of computer code on the planet. As soon as a new supercomputer or parallel array becomes available, there is a climate model waiting to be run on it. It takes the world's fastest computers to keep up with the complexity and detail involved in the latest climate models.

That's because, to get an accurate picture of the world, we need to account for a lot of factors. We need to understand how different types of trees affect their environment, how the deep ocean circulation transports heat around the world, and how a volcanic eruption in the Philippines can cool the entire world for months. Computer modeling allows us to do this precise measurement and analysis.

Dividing the world up into finer and finer grids, climate models today now take into account all the major factors known to affect climate. These include changes in energy from the sun; volcanic eruptions; the effects of different types of clouds and particles in the atmosphere; the influence of forests and fields, water and ice at the earth's surface; heat transport by ocean currents deep below the surface; and, of course, how humans affect the environment.

That's not to say that climate models are a perfect representation of our planet. Of course not! And those who build and run even the most sophisticated models in the world would be the first to say so.

To perfectly simulate the earth, we'd need to know everything about every process, large or small, that occurs on our planet. Our models are limited by our *knowledge*. There are many things that we don't understand and haven't measured. The world God has designed for us is as complex as our own human bodies.

But climate models continue to surprise us with their abilities, as scientists use the models to simulate the past. In this way, they can compare the model results with actual historical records to determine just how accurate the models really are. Often, this comparison identifies ways the models fall short and can be improved. But that's not always the case. In two instances, temperature information from satellites did not agree with the models. Many logically assumed that the models were at fault. But, in both cases, reanalysis of the satellite data revealed that it was actually the satellite data that had been calculated wrongly. The models were closer to the truth than the original "data" had been.

A great deal of meticulous work and incredible detail goes into designing and calibrating climate models. But the results can be very rewarding. Each new insight reveals more about the delicate and complex mechanisms God has put in place to support life on our planet. And these insights provide the information we need to become more aware of the impacts of our actions on our world.

Unequivocal Evidence of Human-Caused Change

Today, twenty-five different global climate models are being run at laboratories around the world. Some are variants of one parent model, while others represent new attempts to capture the complexity of the planet in thousands of lines of computer code.

Contrary to popular belief, these models are *not* based on simple statistical correlations between temperature and greenhouse gases. No, figuring out what is causing this warming is much more complex than drawing a line graph showing temperature and carbon dioxide both going up. After all, that could just be coincidence. Instead, these models are based on fundamental physical principles—conservation of energy and momentum, heat, and pressure. As such, these models are not programmed to produce any specific answer. Rather, scientists feed into them everything we know about changes in the sun, volcanoes, natural cycles, and human production of greenhouse gases, and the models are left to run on their own, come what may.

This is how scientists answer the question, "How do we know *we* are causing the warming?" Using these models, they can create that "earth with no people." This is a virtual world that changes only because of natural causes: volcanic eruptions, changes in the amount of energy the earth is receiving from the sun, natural variability of the climate system, and many other factors. Computer models are run from the mid-1800s to the present. Then the average temperatures of this virtual "earth with no people" can be compared to the real, observed temperatures of the Earth over that same time period.

The same models can then be used to create an "earth with people." This time, the virtual world is permitted to change in response to both natural *and* human-induced increases in greenhouse gas levels.

We can compare the temperature of these two different "earths" to the actual, observed temperature of Earth over that same time period (see Figure 12 in the center insert). On the graph, the red line shows Earth's actual, observed temperatures over the last century. The blue line represents an "earth without people" and shows the average of the temperatures predicted by a number of different climate models. The black line represents a simulated "earth with people."

There's not much difference between the three colored lines for the first half of the 1900s. This tells us that temperature changes over this time were likely driven by a combination of human and natural factors.

However, for the last half of the century, we see a very different picture. Over the land, over the ocean, and over every major continent in the world, there is no way to explain the temperature increases that have been observed if we leave humans out of the equation. In fact, for much of the world, temperatures should actually be *decreasing* if natural causes were the only influence on climate.

The observed increase in greenhouse gas levels, due to human production, is the only explanation we can find to account for what has happened to our world. We've dusted for fingerprints. There's only one likely suspect remaining.

It's us.

8

WE'VE DONE IT BEFORE

"As people of religious faith, we bishops believe that the atmosphere that supports life on earth is a God-given gift, one we must respect and protect. It unites us as one human family. If we harm the atmosphere, we dishonor our Creator and the gift of creation."

—The United States Conference of
Catholic Bishops

Human-induced climate change has been happening for more than a century. Some would argue, much longer than that. But this is not the first time human activities have affected the earth's atmosphere. We've been down this road before.

Learning how we dealt with our previous impacts on the atmosphere can provide us with hope in our current situation. We obviously need some guidance on how to tackle this climate problem. And there's nothing like an encouraging example from the past to help in our time of need.

So what happens when science identifies a critical threat, and the world responds? To answer that question, we'll need to tell you the "hole story."

The Hole Story

Early in the twentieth century, an American engineer named Thomas Midgley made an important discovery. He was able to combine and stabilize chemical substances called chlorofluorocarbons (CFCs) to replace the very poisonous alternative used in refrigerators of the day. Within just a few decades, CFCs were being used everywhere—in air-conditioning units, refrigerators, spray cans, and fire extinguishers.

We didn't know then that CFCs endure for such a long time that they can actually rise all the way to the upper atmosphere. This upper atmosphere is where a thin shield of ozone protects the earth from the sun's cancer-causing rays. Here, CFCs are broken down into chemicals that react with and destroy our protective ozone shield.

Initially, decreases in the ozone shield over the South Pole were chalked up to a mistake in measurement. It wasn't until the 1980s that we found out that the protective ozone layer over the earth's pole was disappearing. And our use of CFCs was to blame.

Thankfully, this problem was identified relatively quickly. Even better, the world responded in record-breaking time. By 1996, nearly every nation in the world had signed an international treaty banning CFCs. As a result, the ozone hole is just beginning to recover today. Full recovery is expected within a few decades.

This problem was much easier to solve, since CFCs were produced in only a small number of ways. And it was relatively simple to find replacements for CFCs quickly—in less than a decade.

Addressing the problem of carbon dioxide and other greenhouse gases will not be so easy. They come from many different sources that are harder to control. But our success with the ozone hole (so far) can serve as encouragement that, working together, we *can* take on a global problem and solve it.

Air Pollution and the Dust Blanket

Another success story—or at least, one on its way to succeeding—is acid rain. Burning fossil fuels doesn't just produce greenhouse gases. It also produces large amounts of sulfur particles and soot.

These particles are serious air pollutants that affect people's health and cause acid rain.

In the months leading up to the Beijing Olympic games in 2008, an enormous amount of media coverage was devoted to analyzing the city's air quality. The media continually showed pictures of the yellow-gray haze overlying the city. That smog and haze was a result of the cars and factories surrounding the city. They produced the same type of particles that we're talking about here—sulfur particles and soot.

Under significant pressure from the athletes, many of whom even threatened not to compete, Beijing took radical steps to reduce its emissions by shutting down factories and limiting car use. In a matter of days, the air cleared and the inhabitants of Beijing were able to get a rare breath of fresh air under a clear blue sky.

So why don't cities in Europe and the Americas look the way Beijing did? A few decades ago, many of them did. London, in particular, was notorious for its poor air quality. Inhabitants began burning sea coal as early as the 1200s, leading to famously bad fogs and poor air quality. As early as 1292, King Edward III announced that anyone caught selling or burning sea coal would be tortured and executed. This sounds severe, but it didn't stop the Londoners for long.

The problem got worse over time even as it spread around the globe. In 1943, the first smog attack in Los Angeles left its inhabitants with burning eyes, nausea, and breathing problems. It was so bad that, at first, people thought it was due to a gas leak from a nearby chemical plant.

In the 1970s, production of sulfur particles from coal-burning power plants was so widespread that it caused acid rain. Acid rain ate away at historic buildings, ruined forests, and killed off entire lakes in the northeastern United States and Canada.

In response to the obvious and visible effects of these air pollutants, the United States, the United Kingdom, and most other developed nations passed laws such as the Clean Air Act. These laws severely limited emissions of these harmful particles; not by cutting fossil fuel use, but by putting filters into smokestacks that would trap these particles before they got into the atmosphere. Today, air pollution and acid rain have been drastically reduced in many places around the world. This is yet another success story that vividly illustrates how something many people once thought was far too expensive and virtually impossible may be easier than anyone imagines, if we just grit our teeth and get started.

Thanks to the Clean Air Act, we even have a thirty-year example of how to go about limiting emissions. A method called "cap and trade" was successfully used to reduce sulfur particle emissions from power plants. The government sets a "cap" limiting what total emissions are allowed to be. Individual companies then reduce their emissions, and anyone who reduces below the required level can then sell or trade those credits to other companies who have not. The very same method can be used to reduce carbon dioxide emissions as well. So you see, although we might not have done much to prevent climate change in the last few decades, we *have* learned a lot about how it can be done.

Global Dimming: How Particles Cooled the Earth

Unfortunately, it's not *all* good news that we've reduced the production of soot and sulfates. That's because these particles are not just air pollutants that harm our health and cause acid rain. They also reflect the sun's energy back to space, actually cooling down the earth.

Over the past century, the presence of these particles has been good news for our climate! The dust and soot we produced masked some of the effects of the increase in greenhouse gases. Yes, it's true. We would have experienced a much greater temperature rise if these particles hadn't been cooling the earth. From 1960 to 1990, it's been estimated that dust, soot, and aerosol particles reduced the amount of solar energy that reached the earth's surface by 4 percent. This effect is known as *global dimming.*

But this counterbalancing act cannot continue. The particles last in the atmosphere only a few days to weeks. Greenhouse gases, in contrast, stay up there for decades to centuries. And now that aerosol particles are being reduced, the heating effect of greenhouse gases has become more pronounced.

For health reasons, we simply cannot afford to keep pumping these cooling particles into the atmosphere. Now, we need to attack the greenhouse gas problem directly. And our success stories with the ozone hole and the earth's dust blanket give us hope that maybe, just maybe, we can succeed.

part three

doubts

9

WEATHER IS NOT CLIMATE

"Climate is what we expect, weather is what we get."
—Mark Twain

The evidence for a warming planet is convincing. But when we hear something in the news about record cold temperatures, or massive snowstorms, it's all too tempting to scoff, "So where's that so-called global *warming* now? I could use a bit of that!"

As humans, we find it difficult to reconcile what our five senses tell us about the weather outside with what scientists are saying about climate change. To understand how exceptionally cold weather and global warming could *both* be happening at the same time, we need to reflect on how our human memory usually functions. We also need to recognize the fundamental difference between weather and climate. That way, we'll be more aware of which signs can serve as evidence that global warming is happening, and which simply cannot.

Short Stories Versus the Long Tale

Memory is a strange phenomenon. It's sometimes hard to remember where you left your keys or the name of the person you just met. At the same time, specific events from decades ago can be etched into your mind forever.

We all have our weather stories. People talk about the winter of '76. "It was so cold," they say, "the lake froze over in October." Or what about the summer of '95, when it was "so hot that you could fry an egg on the sidewalk." Our minds are designed to remember extraordinary events, the ones that stick out as unusual.

For example, the first part of the winter of 2007–2008 was colder than average in the Northern Hemisphere. China experienced its coldest winter since 1985, and Toronto received more snow than any of the previous one hundred years. Katharine's parents, who live in Toronto, sent us a photo of an enormous pile of snow left by the plow with only the tip of an eighteen-foot maple tree poking through the top of the snow pile.

Well, so much for global warming, right?

Wrong.

At the same time that we're having record snowfalls, Earth's temperature has continued to creep upward. We just don't notice it. That's because weather is very different from climate. They are *not* one and the same.

Weather is what our minds are designed to remember. It describes conditions from day to day, week to week, and even from year to year. Weather is that one sweltering week in July, or the coldest November on record, or the snowiest winter ever.

Climate, on the other hand, is nearly impossible for us to remember. It describes the average weather conditions over tens, hundreds, and even thousands of years. Climate is the average temperature or rainfall in a certain place, based on what it's been like for decades.

Many of our relatives in Canada have stories about friends from down South who showed up for a visit in July with skis strapped to the roof of their car. If they had bothered to check the climate of southern Ontario, they would know that summers are usually quite warm and humid, with not a trace of snow in sight. That's climate.

But at the same time, Katharine's great-grandfather used to tell us stories about one July day back in the early 1900s when it *did* snow. Now that's unpredictable weather for you!

To keep track of climate and decide for ourselves if it is changing, we would have to be some type of gifted savant. We'd have to be capable of remembering the temperature and rainfall on every single day of the year for decades at a time. And then we'd have to be able to average all those numbers in our head in order to decide what is normal climate and what is not.

There aren't a lot of people capable of those kinds of mental calculations. So that's why we keep such detailed records. Then we plot them and look at the records of global temperature (see Figure 2). And they clearly show us that, even if we're in the middle of the coldest winter we can remember, global warming is still happening.

The Big Picture

One exceptionally cold year doesn't disprove long-term climate change. But what about some of those places in the world where temperatures *aren't* warming? Doesn't that disprove climate change?

We are already familiar with the difference between global trends versus individual cases in many different areas of life. For example, doctors tell us that if we eat lots of fatty foods, we raise our risk of heart trouble. Now if you take into account the entire population, it's true that those who eat more fatty foods have a higher rate of heart disease.

On the other hand, you have Katharine's grandfather. He's eaten a hearty breakfast of bacon and eggs nearly every day of his life. In addition, he spent most of his life running a gourmet ice cream factory, which of course required frequent taste tests. Well, Grandpa is well into his nineties now, with no sign of any heart trouble. So does that mean that health warnings about fatty foods are unfounded? No, all that means is that he has some pretty lucky genes—genes we hope our children inherit.

Similarly, there are still some individual locations around the world that are fortunate to not be warming yet, even though the rest of the world is warming. Other things are going on at those locations that counteract the effects of global warming. In some places such as the central United States, increased evaporation has absorbed most of the extra heat from global warming. In other places, widespread irrigation has altered local climate.

Individual cases and events, however compelling they may be, aren't at all incompatible with global climate change. They just don't tell the whole story. Global climate change is a change in climate, not weather; and one that is occurring around the world, not in one individual location.

Climate change must be examined "climatically," over time scales of decades to centuries; and globally, by considering as many observations as we have available to us from all around the world.

Climate requires the big picture, long-term view.

Don't Trust the Forecast!

Another popular argument you've probably heard is, "They can't even predict the weather for next week, so how do they justify telling us that they know what it's going to be like in fifty or a hundred years?"

All of us like to complain about how weather forecasts are always wrong. But weather forecasting is a tough job, because weather is inherently chaotic. It's been proven mathematically that it's impossible to predict the weather more than two weeks in advance. And in reality, two weeks is on the optimistic side.

Weather is by nature unpredictable, driven by unforeseeable forces. We all know that. But what many don't know is that climate is relatively predictable, driven by forces we *do* know about.

Here's an example that we can all relate to. Can you say for sure what the temperature will be seven days from now? Probably not. That's weather. If you could produce reliable predictions seven days in advance, you'd be making a lot of money.

Now, can you say whether the month of July in the Northern

Hemisphere will be warmer than the month of January? Yes, we can be nearly certain that it will be. That's climate.

Climate is stable and predictable for decades or even centuries, under a given set of assumptions regarding how much energy we receive from the sun and more recently, what our greenhouse gas emissions are.

Weather, on the other hand, is that one blistering summer, or that record-breaking winter storm, or even that year when every season seemed like it didn't make sense. Weather is inherently unpredictable. Some days are exactly what we expect, while others give us snow when we expect rain, or 80°F when it should be 50°F.

So it's no wonder, if we aren't aware of the fundamental differences between weather and climate, that some doubt scientific claims about climate "prediction."

Think Global

To really be able to judge for ourselves whether climate change is real or not, we've got to focus on the long-term records around the globe, such as those shown in Figure 2. We can't conclude something from our own intuition, personal observations, or memories of weather in our neck of the woods.

Don't let your memory of some recent extremes, whether hot or cold, influence whether you believe global warming is really happening. The reality is that global warming is about long-term changes in climate, measured over many decades or more. It's not about short-term changes that we see in the weather from one day to the next, or even from year to year.

Think global. Think long term. That's where the evidence is found.

10

THE NATURAL WAY OF THINGS

"I'm not one to attribute every activity of man to the changes in the climate. There is something to be said also for man's activities, but also for the cyclical temperature changes on our planet."

—Sarah Palin, Governor of Alaska

There is compelling evidence that the current warming is unprecedented in human history, and that it's happening because of human activity. Still, some continue to argue that what we're witnessing is just the natural way of things. And their arguments tend to cluster around a few common claims:

- "The connection between temperature and carbon dioxide is unclear."
- "We've seen similar cycles before, so this is nothing new."
- "God would never have designed our planet in a way that we could do it damage."

Although each of these arguments has intuitive appeal, the truth is that they don't stand up to the facts. And in this chapter, we'll see why.

Svante Arrhenius and Human Production of Carbon Dioxide

It's difficult to argue with the fact that burning coal, oil, and gas produces carbon dioxide, when we can measure it at a tailpipe or smokestack. And there is no doubt that atmospheric levels of these gases have been increasing—those, too, can be measured with simple instruments. On top of that, the heat-trapping properties of carbon dioxide, methane, and other greenhouse gases are indisputable.

It's been more than a hundred years since scientists first suspected that substantial increases in heat-trapping gases could raise temperatures worldwide. So why has this last link, between carbon dioxide and global temperature, generated such skepticism? Compelling evidence from our climate models shows how an earth without human production of greenhouse gases would actually have been *cooling* rather than warming over the last few decades. But this is not something we can easily calculate for ourselves.

There has been at least one man who did exactly that, though. Starting just before Christmas in 1896, a Swedish scientist named Svante Arrhenius began work on a calculation. Using pen and paper, it took him more than a year to complete. He combined this "simple calculation," as he modestly called it, with his friend Arvid Högbom's findings that burning fossil fuels could increase atmospheric levels of carbon dioxide. Arrhenius found that Arctic temperatures would rise about 14–16°F if carbon dioxide levels increase by two-and-a-half to three times—conditions Arrhenius thought wouldn't be likely to happen for three thousand years or so. Today, we know we are likely to reach that point well before 2100.

Although Arrhenius had to make many simplifying assumptions that today's climate models do not, even still, his calculations were impressive. Recent calculations with sophisticated models verified his work: by the 2090s (when carbon dioxide levels are more than two times the 1890s levels) temperatures are projected to increase 7–13°F over most of Canada, Greenland, and Siberia, with increases up to 18°F over the Arctic Ocean.

This impressive example demonstrates that the link between increasing carbon dioxide levels and global temperature is based on science that has been around for well over one hundred years. So why all the fuss?

The Chicken or the Egg?

Despite the physical science linking increases in heat-trapping gases to rising temperatures, some still argue that: (1) there is no historical precedent for carbon dioxide driving temperature changes, and therefore, (2) it cannot be doing so today.

The assumption tacit to this line of reasoning is that if temperatures are rising (for some unknown reason), then they are doing so independently of carbon dioxide. Carbon dioxide and other greenhouse gases are just following suit rather than leading the hand. So, in the end, there's nothing we can do about all of this warming. We just have to wait it out.

Within this line of reasoning, there is a partial truth. So, first, let's look at the true part.

Scientists believe that the last ice age ended thousands of years ago when Earth's orbit shifted, altering the distribution of sunlight received by the earth. Temperatures rose a few degrees over several hundred years, with little or no change in greenhouse gases. So, as far as we can tell, it is indeed true that greenhouse gases have never *initiated* a climate warming before.

Now, for the rest of the truth. That initial temperature change caused by the sun was only one-third of the total temperature difference between that ice age and today. So what caused the rest of the warming? The answer is: carbon dioxide and other greenhouse gases.

A temperature change of a few degrees, caused by a small increase in energy from the sun, was not enough to melt all that ice. But it was enough to melt *some* of the ice and slow down the ocean's circulation. Carbon dioxide then built up in the ocean and scientists believe it was released suddenly via two massive "burps" into the atmosphere. Together, these carbon dioxide burps raised the atmospheric levels by about one hundred parts per million. This enhanced the original temperature increase, caused by the sun, by a factor of three.

So the truth is that increases in carbon dioxide and other heat-trapping gases *have* caused temperatures to increase in the past. And realizing this has many scientists worried. If just a slight warming caused by the sun could be amplified threefold by natural carbon dioxide "burps" way back then, what might happen today?

Natural Cycles?

All of us have probably heard someone say at one time or another, "We're just in another cycle and there have been lots of natural cycles throughout the earth's history in the past. So there's nothing to worry about."

Many of these same people who argue for natural cycles also believe in a young Earth. But what we usually *don't* hear is that the natural cycles argument hinges entirely on believing in an old earth. It's impossible to believe in a relatively young Earth and natural cycles at the same time.

As we saw in Figure 7, today's temperatures are already unusual in the context of the last two thousand years. Using "natural thermometers," it's possible to go back even further than that. And when we do so, the picture doesn't change one bit. You can see for yourself in Figure 14, which shows Earth's temperature and the atmosphere's carbon dioxide levels going back six thousand years. If anything, we have been cooling slightly over the last six thousand years—until the last century, that is. But *there have been no major natural cycles in Earth's temperature and greenhouse gases over that time, and no conditions that compare to today.*

It is only with the beginning of the Industrial Era in the 1800s that we see sudden, large increases in carbon dioxide, followed by temperature increases. So the idea of a younger Earth is not compatible with the argument that it's just a natural cycle. There are no natural cycles over the last six thousand years anywhere near the magnitude of what is happening today.

Well, what if we *are* comfortable with the idea of an Earth that is millions of years old? Then, does the "it's just a natural cycle" argument work?

Actually—no, it doesn't even work then.

Over time scales that assume an older Earth, records show that the earth does undergo very large natural cycles, from frozen ice ages to warm interglacial periods. But today, our temperature is at the very upper end of the range of what is normal for any of those cycles. And even more telling, since the 1800s our levels of carbon dioxide and other greenhouse gases in the atmosphere have soared far beyond any levels seen during these natural cycles.

So even the natural cycles tell us that the conditions we are seeing today are extremely unusual circumstances in the context of Earth's history.

Our Freedom and God's Sovereignty

For many of us, a natural reaction to all of this could be to throw up our hands and ask, "How could God have set the world up to function in such a way that normal, everyday activities upset the balance of the earth and cause harm?"

First, it's certainly not an insult to God's omnipotence, as some might claim, to say that the world's climate can be affected by our puny actions. The world around us is affected by our actions every day. Although we are small in scale compared to our giant planet, there is power in numbers.

At the time of Christ, it is estimated that the population of the world was somewhere around 170 million people. By the beginning of the Industrial Revolution in 1750, that number had only grown to 800 million. After that, it took just 250 years for the world's population to soar past 6 billion. With so many people living in the world, it isn't that hard to imagine how our actions today are affecting the planet as a whole.

We also need to recognize that we live in a fallen world. It didn't begin that way. God created a world without pain, without sin, without death. One of the first things we learn about Adam and Eve is that through their actions, they altered the fate of the entire planet. In Romans 8:20–21, Paul tells us, "Against its will, all creation was subjected to God's curse" (NLT). When Adam sinned, it wasn't just humans who fell. It was the planet as well.

God is omnipotent, but He allows things to happen because He refuses to control us. And when it comes to the physical world, God has set up a system whereby tornadoes can rip through towns, hurricanes can wipe out cities, and humans can accidentally alter the balance of the entire planet. But we shouldn't blame God. Lamentations 3:33 tells us, "For He does not willingly bring affliction or grief to any human being" (TNIV). When it comes to climate change, *we* are the authors. Not God.

Climate change would never have been an issue if the creation never fell. But it did, and now we are left to cope with the effects of the Fall, both spiritually and physically.

No miraculous intervention has yet taken place to cool down the earth, and we should not bank on the fact that it will. That's not to say that we believe in a remote God, one who has set up the universe to run like a clock and now lives somewhere far away, uninvolved with our lives. No, the creative and sustaining God we believe in is still intimately involved in every second of the world. And it is perfectly possible that He may give us some help.

For example, some have speculated recently that we may be

heading into a random period of lower energy from the sun, called a "Maunder Minimum," last seen during the late 1600s. If this happened to be true, it would certainly be a blessing. But even this unusual event would reduce the amount of energy the earth receives by the equivalent of seven years' worth of our carbon dioxide emissions. So it would give us a temporary reprieve. But it would not fix the problem. We created the problem, and all indications are that we are also the ones who will have to fix it.

11

NO MORE DEBATE

"I've worked with hundreds of the world's scientists and the vast majority...know that it is happening and understand the science. The basic science after all is very old science; it's been known for two hundred years that we are as warm as we are at the moment because of greenhouse gases. If you put up more of those gases, the world becomes warmer. There is no doubt about that from a physics point of view or from a basic science point of view. No scientist who knows anything will dispute that."

—Sir John Houghton, Chief Executive at the
United Kingdom Meteorological Office and
Co-chair of the Intergovernmental Panel
on Climate Change Scientific Assessment
Working Group (Ret'd.)

Do most climate scientists agree about global warming and its causes? The short answer to this question is an emphatic, *yes*, they do.

Nearly every scientist who publishes in and understands this field of study agrees that climate is changing and that it is primarily because of human activity. And here are the facts to prove it.

An International Consensus

Scientists *love* to argue. You probably couldn't get a roomful of scientists to agree on the exact color of the sky, let alone the state of the planet.

That only makes the degree of scientific consensus on the subject of climate change even more extraordinary. It's true that scientific discussions still continue, hammering out the finer details of what we know about Earth's climate; and these arguments will probably continue for centuries. But today, scientific disagreements center around details: what are the microscale processes by which different types of particles accumulate water? What is the correct way to compare the effects of reducing carbon dioxide versus methane? Or, most seriously, why have our models grossly underestimated the speed at which the Arctic's sea ice and Greenland's ice sheets are melting? These are the types of questions that remain.

In contrast, there is widespread agreement that:

- The global warming observed over the last century—and particularly the last fifty years—is highly unusual.
- Present-day conditions are outside the range of any natural cycles experienced over the course of human civilization.
- Although changes in the sun, volcanoes, and natural cycles continue to affect climate today, the temperature increases we've seen over the last fifty years or more are primarily the result of human production of heat-trapping greenhouse gases.

Who agrees with these statements? First and foremost, the Intergovernmental Panel on Climate Change (IPCC) does. The IPCC is the scientific body whose task is to assess the latest scientific literature relevant to understanding human-induced climate change.

To understand climate change and its impacts, experts from many different areas are needed, from atmospheric scientists to economists. The IPCC is made up of more than two thousand such experts from a broad range of scientific disciplines. Not all are climate scientists, so not all are qualified to judge whether or not climate change is happening, or if it is occurring because of human activities. But each has an individual specialty to contribute to the big picture: how cloud particles are formed, which plant species are most sensitive to climate change, how energy efficiency might be increased in the future, which economic mechanisms might be used to reduce our carbon dioxide emissions.

The reports issued by the IPCC every five years or so represent the most thoroughly reviewed documents in the history of science. And as a group, the latest series of these reports, released in 2007, concluded this:

> Warming of the climate system is unequivocal, as is now evident from observations. Most of the observed increase in global average temperatures since the mid-20th century is very likely due to the observed increase in anthropogenic [human] greenhouse gas concentrations.

The IPCC is not the only organization of scientists to reach a consensus on the human contribution to climate change. In 2008, the United States Climate Change Science Program, created by the George W. Bush administration to address "unresolved questions regarding climate change and global warming," concluded: "It is well established...that the global warming of the past 50 years is due primarily to human-induced increases in heat-trapping gases."

The National Academies of Science of thirty-two nations, including the United States, Canada, and the United Kingdom, have all issued statements agreeing with this conclusion. In the United States, similar assertions have been made by every scientific organization whose members include experts in climate change. These include the American Geophysical Union, the American Institute of Physics, the American Meteorological Society, and the American Association for the Advancement of Science, which declared in 2006:

The scientific evidence is clear: global climate change caused by human activities is occurring now, and it is a growing threat to society. Accumulating data from across the globe reveal a wide array of effects: rapidly melting glaciers, destabilization of major ice sheets, increases in extreme weather, rising sea level, shifts in species ranges, and more. The pace of change and the evidence of harm have increased markedly over the last five years. The time to control greenhouse gas emissions is now.

Even the last holdout, the American Association of Petroleum Geologists, released a statement in 2008 acknowledging the effect humans are having on their environment.

Today, there is no legitimate national or international scientific organization that does not accept the fundamental role of humans as drivers of recent climate change.

An Overwhelming Consensus

It's not just the large scientific organizations that agree on how human activities are affecting our planet. The same consensus is also evident in the scientific literature, and among individual scientists themselves.

The overwhelming agreement among scientists on the issue of global warming was driven home in 2004 by a study conducted by a science historian. She pored over all of the scientific journals from 1993 to 2003, looking for any papers that contained the words *climate change* somewhere in their descriptions or titles. She divided the papers she found into four groups. Group one were papers that said climate change is happening, and most of it is because of human emissions of greenhouse gases. Group two included papers that simply presented analytical methods and didn't say anything about climate change *per se*. Articles in group three looked at climate change in the distant past. And group four was for papers that explicitly rejected the idea that climate change was happening, or that it was occurring because of human emissions.

Surprisingly, at least considering the perception of scientific disagreement often fostered by the media, she found that no scientific papers at all belonged in group four. Independent attempts to replicate her findings, published as an unreviewed report rather than a peer-reviewed journal article, could only categorize one single article in group four.

In other words, from 1993 to 2003 there was essentially no evidence in the peer-reviewed scientific research to support the myth that there is still a major disagreement among scientists regarding the reality and causes of recent climate change. Instead, an overwhelming consensus emerged—less than 0.1 percent of the research in climate science disagreed with the scientific consensus of the IPCC and other international scientific bodies.

These results are bolstered by a 2009 poll conducted by researchers at the University of Illinois Chicago that asked active researchers in the field whether they believed human activity was a significant factor in changing global temperatures. More than 97 percent replied that they agreed, and the survey concluded: "It seems that the debate on the authenticity of global warming and the role played by human activity is largely nonexistent among those who understand the nuances and scientific basis of long-term climate processes."

Disagreements and Debates

That's not to say that there aren't still scientists out there who continue to voice their disagreement with these findings. And—at least at first glance—some of these scientists have impressive credentials. But what's important to realize is that these scientists, while they may be outstanding experts in their own fields, are *not climate scientists*. They do not conduct or publish research in the field of climate science. And because of this, their opinions may often be based on one or more of the erroneous ideas that we have discussed so far.

For example, some of the most frequent doubters are weather

forecasters and meteorologists. As we have seen, weather is inherently very different from climate. Weather is unpredictable and chaotic. And so some meteorologists and weather forecasters question our ability to detect and project human-caused climate change. A few geologists, accustomed to looking at time scales on the order of millions of years, doubt that any short-term changes will be significant. A handful of others, the occasional astronomer or physicist, emphasize the uncertainty and chaotic nature of the climate system, and the predominant role of the sun in controlling past climate. Engineers sometimes assume a key factor has been omitted from climate change calculations, a factor that would provide an alternate explanation for the warming. But none of these arguments stand up to scientific scrutiny.

In 1998 and again in 2007, a petition was circulated that collected more than thirty-one thousand signatures. Based on this petition, the originators claimed that these signatures represented scientists who "declare that global warming is a lie with no scientific basis whatsoever." Questions have been raised concerning the legitimacy of many of these signatures. But even still, here's the truth. The petition asked people to sign if they agreed that "there is no convincing scientific evidence that human release of carbon dioxide, methane, or other greenhouse gases is causing or will, in the foreseeable future, *cause catastrophic heating of the Earth's atmosphere* and disruption of the Earth's climate" (italics ours).

The petition makes no mention of global warming, although an article circulated with the petition defined global warming as "severe increases in Earth's atmospheric and surface temperatures, with disastrous environmental consequences."

Catastrophes have certainly occurred in the history of the earth. These are usually events that have wiped out entire towns, cities, and even civilizations. Major droughts are thought to have led to the downfall and eventual extinction of the Mayan and

Akkadian civilizations, events that would be called catastrophes for the people of those towns and civilizations.

By that measure, nothing like that has yet happened to Earth as a whole. And, at least for humans, a disaster that would wipe out the entire human race is not forecast in the foreseeable future either—insofar as the future is foreseeable, of course.

Few would argue that what we are seeing today is "catastrophic heating." But disagreeing with the statement above does not equal dismissing climate change as a farce.

The Reality of Climate Change

There is no question that it is warmer today than any time in the historical record, and that most of that change is because of human activity. There is no evidence to support the existence of a scientific, fact-based debate regarding the reality of our warming planet and the contributions humans have made to that warming. Instead, concern is growing that science has *underestimated* the rate of change.

When it warmed at other times in history, natural phenomena drove temperatures up over long periods of time. And Earth had time to adapt. Now, human activities are causing change at extraordinary speeds. And scientists are convinced that if we continue on our current pattern of energy use, we can expect global temperature changes on the order of 10°F or more in just one hundred years' time.

Our planet cannot keep up with this unprecedented speed of change, and neither can we. As Christians who care about God's creation, we need to consider the impact our actions are having on our planet.

We have already seen some major changes. These changes are already affecting those on the edges, such as the Inupiaq of Kivalina. But over the coming century, the effects of climate change will touch us all.

12

A WINDOW TO OUR CLIMATE FUTURE

"We cannot predict precisely what will happen, but the coming century promises climatic upheavals the likes of which human beings have not seen since we were hunting mammoths during the ice ages."

—World Vision Australia

Yes, the world is getting warmer. And we are seeing some serious effects in certain places already. But the last doubt that many have is this: How on earth can we tell what's going to happen in the future? And if we don't know what's going to happen, what reason do we have to do things any differently?

Possible Futures: The Science of Climate Change

It's impossible to predict the future. No one can do that. But in the case of climate change, the main reason we can't predict the future is because it depends on the energy choices we make over the next few decades.

If we continue to use gas in our cars and burn coal to generate electricity, we will produce more and more greenhouse gases. More greenhouse gas emissions would mean a relatively larger temperature change over the coming century.

On the other hand, we can find other ways to power our industries, heat our homes, and run our cars. We can use energy from the sun or the wind. We could greatly reduce our dependence on fossil fuels, and hence our production of greenhouse gases. This reduction would certainly mean a smaller increase in temperature over the coming century.

Scientists can develop projections concerning how much climate is likely to change given a set of assumptions about the future. In other words, they can answer the question "What if humans acted in *this* way?" as opposed to "What if humans acted in *that* way?"

Whether or not those choices are made is up to us. But what we *can* do is explore the implications of choices we might make, to see what kind of world those choices would leave for our children.

Scientific Scenarios and Models

In developing these pictures of the future, scientists begin with estimates of how population is likely to grow. Will population continue to increase rapidly, or will its growth slow down over time?

Next, they look at technology. What kind of cars will we be driving (or flying) in the future? How will we be lighting our houses and keeping ourselves warm in the winter?

Last, they look at energy. Will we continue to depend on fossil fuels like coal, oil, and gas to supply most of our energy needs? Or will we replace these with renewable energy sources like wind, solar power, and hydropower?

Through asking these kinds of questions, it is possible to develop a broad range of scenarios, pictures of what the future might be like. Some "higher" scenarios—the ones that show higher greenhouse gas emissions over the coming century—explore what would happen if the world's population more than doubles relative to today, and if we continue to use fossil fuels the same way we have over the last century.

In contrast, the "lower" scenarios—the ones that show large

reductions in greenhouse gas emissions over the coming century, compared to today's levels—explore what would happen if our technology develops rapidly, and we start getting more and more of our energy from renewable sources.

A final category, called a "commitment" scenario, explores what would happen if we were able to freeze atmospheric greenhouse gases at the level they were at in 2000. Though unrealistic, this type of scenario shows us the minimum amount of climate change that we should expect over the coming century.

For each of these different scenarios, scientists calculate the emissions of greenhouse gases that would be produced each year from now until the end of the century. Estimates of future greenhouse gas emissions can then be used as input to the same climate models that have already been tested against past climate observations. Once scientists are confident that their models are able to reproduce what's already happened in the world over the last century, then the models can be used to study what would be likely to happen in the future under a given scenario such as those described above.

Possible Futures: Higher or Lower

The results of climate model calculations based on these future scenarios are summarized in Figure 13 in the center insert. This figure shows the change in global temperature that would be expected over the rest of this century. Projected changes are shown for three different future scenarios: higher emissions, lower emissions, and the carbon dioxide level "freeze."

If we continue to produce increasing amounts of greenhouse gases over the next century, temperature change will be greater than under a scenario where we reduce our emissions.

If emissions continue to increase, for example, global temperatures could increase by 6–13°F by the end of the century. If we can significantly reduce our greenhouse gas emissions, by 2100, temperatures could still increase by 2–6°F over the same time period. And even if we managed to "freeze" levels of carbon dioxide in the atmosphere, we would still see a temperature increase of around 1°F by the end of the century relative to today.

These future calculations are still limited by our imperfect understanding of our complex planet. That's what creates the range of temperatures expected under a given scenario. But at the same time these calculations give us three very important pieces of information:

1. The temperature changes we've already seen over the last century are only a fraction of what can be expected over this century. Even under a best-case scenario, we will still experience twice the temperature change in the next hundred years as we did in the last.

2. Our *choices* are the most important factor in determining what future climate will be like. Depending on whether emissions are higher or lower, we could see temperature changes of just a degree or two, or more than ten degrees.

3. Temperature changes could be even higher than projected here, if Earth reacts as it has in the past to warming temperatures, by releasing large amounts of natural greenhouse gases into the atmosphere.

If We Had to Bet...

So to review, the two largest uncertainties affecting where (on the scale shown in Figure 13) our planet will end up by the end of this century are:

1. The choices we make that affect our production of greenhouse gases today, and over the next few decades.
2. How Earth responds to those changes.

It's too early to answer those questions today—again, no one can predict the future. But we *can* look to what has happened over the last decade or more for clues. Has our production of greenhouse gases been on the higher or the lower end of these scenarios? How quickly is the planet responding to recent changes? Has natural production of greenhouse gases changed at all in response to warming temperatures?

And when we do look at the last decade, the news is not good.

Today, worldwide production of greenhouse gases is higher even than that estimated under the "higher" scenario shown in Figure 13. That means that, in terms of human choices, we may be already on our way to a future characterized by a temperature change faster and greater in magnitude than any currently imagined.

At the same time, increasing amounts of carbon dioxide and methane are also being released into the atmosphere from natural sources. It's estimated that the frozen Arctic tundra holds the equivalent of one thousand years' worth of greenhouse gas production, at today's levels. Large "burps" of methane have already been sighted bubbling out of bogs and lakes in Siberia and northern Canada, as the ground defrosts. If the planetary warming continues to accelerate, as much as 10 percent of that could be released by the end of the century. This would effectively double the consequences of human production over the same time period.

Over the last century, the ocean has been making up for some of our human production of carbon dioxide by absorbing more carbon dioxide than it produces. This has made it more acidic, and hence less able to absorb increasing amounts of carbon. In addition, warmer temperatures are driving stronger winds over the oceans. Stronger winds are exposing deeper layers of water, already saturated with carbon. Together, these two factors are reducing the amount of carbon dioxide the oceans are absorbing. This means that more is staying in the atmosphere, increasing its effect even further.

FIGURE 1 Kivalina: America's First Climate Refugees

Every year, the ocean eats away more of Kivalina's narrow shoreline. The coastline was once protected by thick ice. Now, warming temperatures due to climate change are causing the protective ice to form later and later in the year. As the erosion continues, this Alaska village needs $150 million or more to relocate inland—money they do not have.

FIGURE 2 Earth's Average Temperature Is Rising

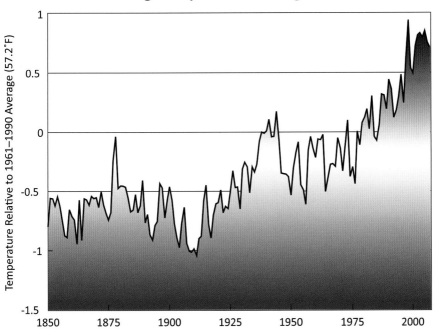

The calculation of Earth's average temperature is based on observations from thousands of locations around the world. Here, temperature changes are shown relative to the global average temperature for the period 1961–1990. Over the last century, global average temperatures have risen steadily despite year-to-year variations.

FIGURE 3 Temperature in Central England: 350 Years of Records

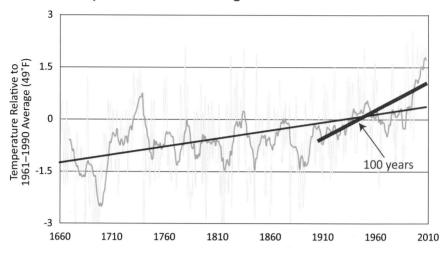

The world's oldest continuous thermometer record of monthly temperatures is from central England. This record mirrors the upward trend of average global temperatures. Annual average temperatures vary from year to year (pale orange line), while 10-year average temperatures show longer-term trends (dark orange line). Temperatures have increased over the entire record (red line). However, the increase in the last 100 years is much steeper than in the past (brown line).

FIGURE 4 The Truth of Warming: No Cooling in Sight

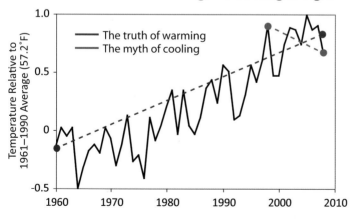

The key to climate change lies in trends over 30 years or more. The long red line shows 50 years of global temperature increase. The short blue line shows the temperature difference between two points, 1998 and 2008, chosen to provide the illusion that global warming is slowing or has stopped. In fact, 1998 was a particularly warm El Niño year, while 2008 was a relatively cool La Niña year. Such short-term natural variability does not negate the truth of the long-term warming trend.

FIGURE 5 Warming Is Global:
Not Due to Local Urban Heat Island Effects

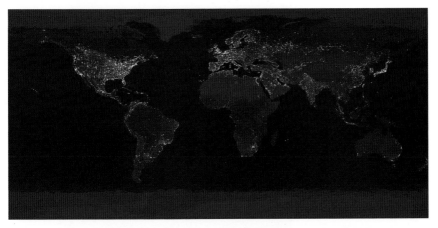

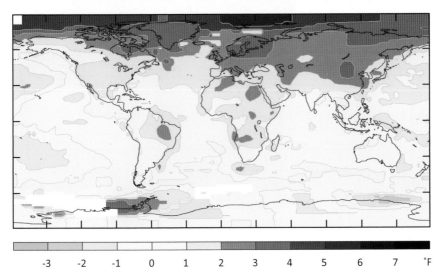

Global warming cannot be an artifact of the urban heat island effect. If it were, warming would happen over large urban centers. Instead, the greatest warming is taking place over largely uninhabited regions. This can be seen by comparing this photograph of the Earth at night (top panel) with a map showing areas where the fastest warming has taken place over the last 30 years, relative to the long-term average (bottom panel). The greatest warming has not occurred in the lighted areas, where most of the Earth's people live and where the urban heat island effect is greatest. Instead, the Earth has warmed faster in areas such as the Arctic, Greenland, and Siberia, where few people live. Warming has also occurred over the oceans.

FIGURE 6 Tree Rings: A Look Back in Time

As trees grow, their rings preserve records of the temperature and rainfall conditions experienced during each year of the tree's life. Tree-ring data from around the world can be pieced together to produce records of climate conditions, extending back thousands of years. Here, Andrew points at a redwood tree trunk from Muir Woods National Monument that is nearly 1,000 years old. White lines show the timing of important events in U.S. history, such as Columbus discovering America and the signing of the Declaration of Independence.

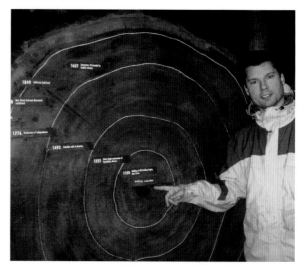

FIGURE 7 Northern Hemisphere Temperature from 200 to 2008 A.D.

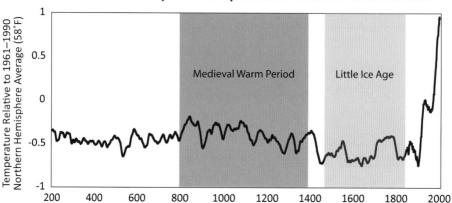

The average temperature in the Northern Hemisphere can be pieced together all the way back to the year 200 A.D., based on "natural thermometer" records from written records, tree rings, coral reefs, lake sediments, and ice cores. Despite natural variations in climate that caused the Medieval Warm Period and the Little Ice Age, this record clearly shows that the increase in temperatures observed over the last century is unprecedented in the context of human civilization over the last 2,000 years.

FIGURE 8 100 Years of Carbon Dioxide Emissions

Contribution to
Global Carbon Dioxide
Emissions 1900–2002

- <0.01%
- 0.01% to 0.1%
- 0.1% to 1%
- 1% to 7%
- 8% (China, Russia)
- 30% (USA)

When we add up each nation's production of carbon dioxide over the last century, it is obvious that certain countries have contributed more than others to the buildup of carbon dioxide in the atmosphere. From 1900 to 2004, the U.S. contributed 30% of the global total of carbon dioxide. China and Russia each contributed less than 8%. Most countries in Africa and Latin America contributed less than 1% each.

FIGURE 9 Human Sources of Greenhouse Gases

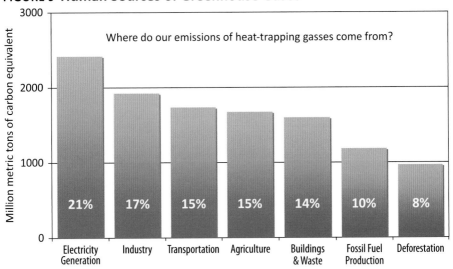

Examining one year's greenhouse gas emissions shows us how production of these heat-trapping gases is woven throughout the fabric of our society. Major sources come from powering our industry, our cars, and our homes. Agriculture, deforestation, and waste also contribute. These numbers represent global emissions. In the United States, the top sources are electricity generation (34%), transportation (27%), and industry (20%).

FIGURE 10 The Sun Is Not the Cause of Current Climate Change

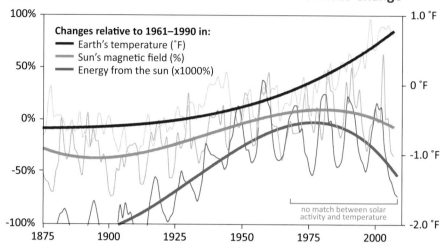

Increases in energy from the sun likely contributed to warming over the first half of the 1900s. However, if the sun were controlling Earth's temperature today, our temperatures would have decreased over the last few decades. Instead, they have increased.

FIGURE 11 Carbon Dioxide Emissions and Atmospheric Levels, 1800 to 2005

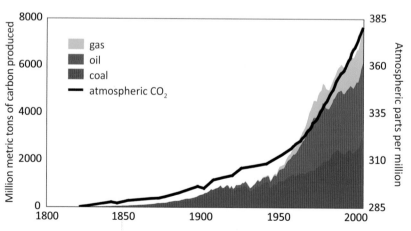

Production of carbon dioxide from burning coal, oil, and natural gas has increased exponentially since the beginning of the Industrial Era, causing atmospheric levels of carbon dioxide (CO_2) to rise from 285 to 385 parts per million.

FIGURE 12 Climate Models: Reliably Reproducing Human Impact on Climate

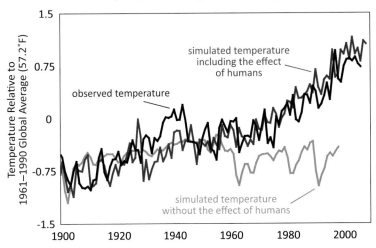

Climate models are the most helpful and scientifically reliable tools available to examine causes of climate change. We can compare observed global temperatures (black line) with climate model simulations of temperature that include human production of heat-trapping gases (red line), and those that do not include human influence (blue line). Only when climate model simulations include human influence are they able to account for the global temperature increase since 1960.

FIGURE 13 Global Temperature 1900 to 2100: Up and Up

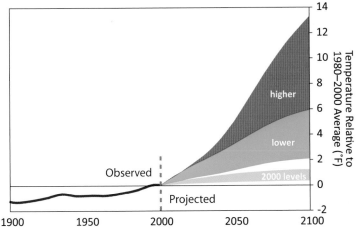

Global temperatures have already risen by 1.4°F since the beginning of the Industrial Era. However, much greater changes are expected over the rest of this century. If atmospheric levels of carbon dioxide could somehow be frozen at 2000 levels (green area), we would still see an additional 0.5 to 1°F warming. If our production of heat-trapping gases is significantly reduced (blue area), we can still expect a warming on the order of 2 to 6°F. If we continue to depend on fossil fuels for our energy (orange area), temperature changes are likely to be much greater, on the order of 6 to 13°F.

FIGURE 14 Carbon Dioxide and Temperature: An Unnatural High

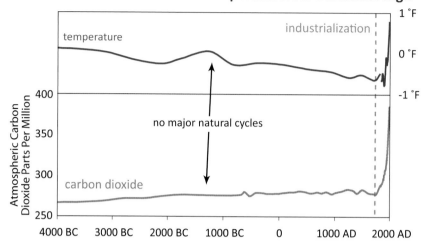

Natural thermometers extend our temperature records back many thousands of years. Average temperatures based on natural records (red line) show that temperatures have cooled slightly over the last 6,000 years, and that carbon dioxide levels in the atmosphere (blue line) have remained relatively constant. Not until the beginning of the Industrial Era do carbon dioxide levels and temperature begin a startling rise.

FIGURE 15 Air Bubbles in Ice Preserve Records of Past Climate

Tiny bubbles of air, trapped in polar ice, provide natural records of air temperature and levels of heat-trapping gases in the atmosphere from the time the ice was formed. Scientists travel to Greenland and Antarctica to drill long cores of ice, and count the layers back in time. Here, Rebecca Anderson from Nevada's Desert Research Institute examines a section of an ice core retrieved from nearly 1,700 feet below the surface of the West Antarctic Ice Sheet. This ice core holds information on the Earth's temperature and its atmosphere from a very long time ago.

FIGURE 16 Extremely Hot Days: More Frequent and Widespread

historical (1961–1990)

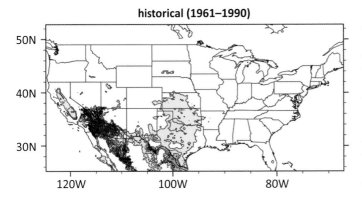

lower emissions (2070–2099)

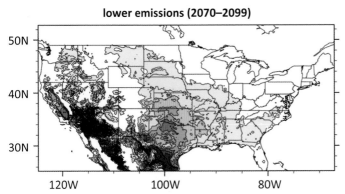

higher emissions (2070-2099)

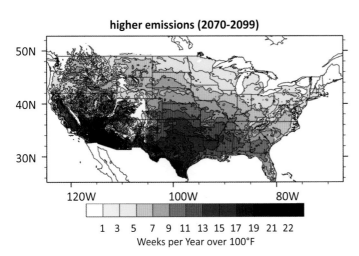

1 3 5 7 9 11 13 15 17 19 21 22
Weeks per Year over 100°F

Climate change means that some extremes, such as very hot days, are becoming more frequent, and even more extreme. Currently, only a few locations in the southwest U.S. experience more than seven days each year with temperatures above 100°F. By the end of the century, much of the south and central U.S. could experience these types of conditions, even if our emissions are reduced. If we do not reduce our production of heat-trapping gases, before the end of the century the entire country could experience weeks of these extreme heat days each year.

FIGURE 17 Warmer Temperatures: Stronger Hurricanes

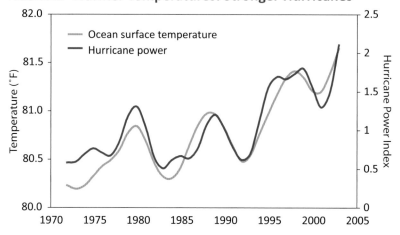

The power of hurricanes increases as the ocean's surface warms. Here, the average hurricane power index for Atlantic and Pacific storms shows how increases in hurricane power have paralleled increases in Atlantic and Pacific Ocean temperatures over the last few decades. Although the actual number of hurricanes has not changed greatly, the number of Category 4 and 5 storms doubled from 1970 to 2004. As climate change continues to heat the oceans, we can expect even greater numbers of strong hurricanes in the future.

FIGURE 18 Hurricane Rita and Warm Ocean Waters

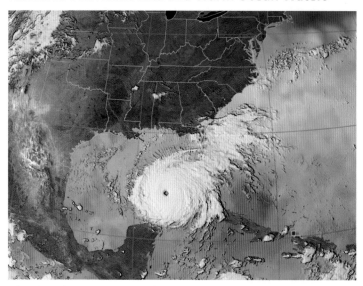

A hurricane becomes stronger the more time it spends over warm ocean waters. This map shows Hurricane Rita at its maximum as a Category 5 storm on September 21, 2005. Under the hurricane you can see the warm ocean waters of the Gulf of Mexico. Waters just 1°F warmer than usual increased the hurricane's wind speeds by a few percent, providing the storm with energy to grow into a Category 5 hurricane.

FIGURE 19 More Frequent Heat Waves and Droughts: Southeastern Australia in 2009

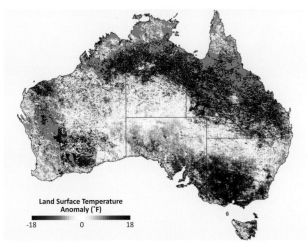

Land Surface Temperature Anomaly (°F)

-18 0 18

Climate change is already leading to longer and more severe heat waves, droughts, and heavy rainfall events. Although no single extreme event can be attributed to climate change alone, the unprecedented events experienced by Australia in early 2009 are certainly consistent with our picture of a warming world. During the week of January 25, northern Australia experienced record rains, flooding, and below-average temperatures. At the same time, temperatures in southern Australia soared to nearly 20°F above average for days on end. This heat wave, occurring on top of the longest drought in Australian history, created the ideal conditions for the devastating wildfires that ripped through the region.

FIGURE 20 Worsening Drought in Central Africa

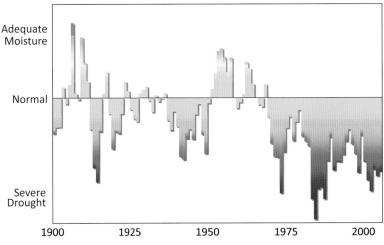

Droughts are getting longer and stronger in many parts of the world. Central Africa has experienced relentless drought conditions since the 1970s. This drying is caused by warmer ocean waters in the Indian Ocean. Although parts of Africa are starting to recover from this drought, climate change is projected to send other areas, such as the U.S. Southwest, into near-permanent dust bowl conditions over the coming century.

FIGURE 21 Melting Glaciers in the United States:
Glacier National Park in 1913 and 2005

In Montana, 150 glaciers originally existed in Glacier National Park. Today, 27 glaciers remain, including the Shepard Glacier shown above. All the remaining glaciers are shrinking rapidly. Within 20 years, the park will likely have no glaciers left.

This decline in ice and snow is consistent across most of the western United States, where shrinking snowpack has been definitively linked to human-caused warming. More precipitation is falling as rain, and less as snow. This is bad news for farmers such as those in California, who depend on melting snow in the Sierra Nevada Mountains for much of their water supply. If our production of heat-trapping gases continues, more than 80% of the snowpack these farmers rely on for irrigation could be gone before the end of the century.

FIGURE 22 Melting Glaciers Worldwide:
Peruvian Glaciers in 1978 and 2004

The Quelccaya Ice Cap in the Peruvian Andes is the primary source of water for the city of Lima's 8 million people. It has shrunk by 30% in the last 30 years. These images, both taken in July, show the Qori Kalis glacier that leads out of the Quelccaya Ice Cap. This glacier is now melting 10 times faster than before, and is likely to disappear within just a few years. Most glaciers in the Himalayas and Andes will be gone within a matter of decades, threatening water supplies for over a billion people in Southeast Asia and many millions in South America. These people depend on glacier melt-water for drinking, irrigating their crops, and generating hydroelectric power.

FIGURE 23 The Arctic: Shrinking Summer Sea Ice

Arctic summer sea ice has been decreasing steadily since satellite observations began in 1979. All-time record lows were broken in 2005 and again in 2007. Scientists estimate the summer Arctic could be ice-free within just a few years, opening the Northwest Passage to shipping and resource exploration. While melting sea ice doesn't change global sea levels directly, it does have serious implications for regional climate change. Dark waters absorb much more heat than bright white ice. Thus, melting sea ice causes the Arctic to warm even faster, speeding up the melting of Greenland's land ice, which does lead to significant sea level rise.

FIGURE 24 Greenland in 1979 and 2007: Greater and Faster Melting

A much greater area of Greenland's ice surface is now melting, when compared to the first satellite observations in 1979. Unlike sea ice, melt-water from land-based ice, such as that on Greenland, directly contributes to sea level rise. If all of Greenland were to melt, sea level would rise by about 23 feet, endangering major cities such as New York, Miami, and Los Angeles. Although it would take several centuries for Greenland to melt entirely, enough warming could occur in this century to make its eventual meltdown inevitable.

FIGURE 25 Sea Level Rise 1900 to 2100: Up and Up

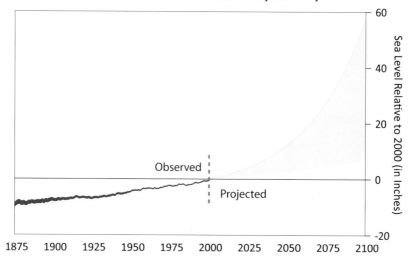

Sea level has risen 10 inches over the past century, mostly due to the expansion of warming ocean water. Over the last few decades, sea level rise has accelerated. This acceleration is happening because land-based ice sheets and glaciers are melting faster, adding more water to the world's oceans. During this century, sea level could rise from 7 to nearly 60 inches, depending on how quickly Greenland and other ice sheets melt.

FIGURE 26 Coastal Areas at Risk from Sea Level Rise

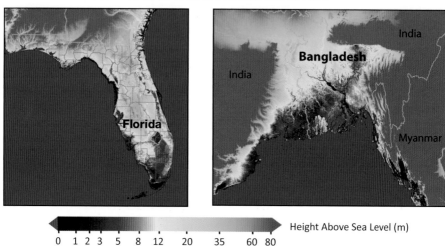

More than 10% of the world's population lives in low-lying coastal areas that are extremely vulnerable to climate change. The most vulnerable areas include the tightly-packed coastal areas of Asia and Africa, and small island states. By the end of this century, the nation of Bangladesh could lose 17% of its land area and half of its rice fields to sea level rise due to climate change. The island nation of Tuvalu could lose its entire country. In the United States, low-lying areas like Florida and Louisiana are at particular risk. However, all coastlines will experience more flooding and erosion. Some cities, such as New York, are already planning for the effects of rising sea level.

FIGURE 27 Climate Change Deaths: An Average of 150,000 Per Year

The World Health Organization estimates that 150,000 people die every year from illnesses and injuries related to climate change. The effects of climate change fall disproportionately on the poor and vulnerable, who cannot protect themselves from extreme temperatures, flooding, and disruptions to their food and water supplies.

FIGURE 28 10 Slices of Carbon Pie: How to Reduce Global Emissions

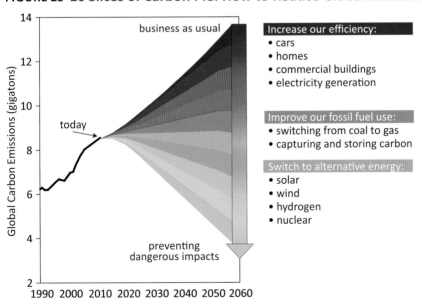

Globally, our emissions must be reduced at least 60% by 2050 in order to prevent the most dangerous impacts of climate change. These reductions can be achieved in ten areas, in most cases using existing technology that must now be widely applied. A reduction of this magnitude would still result in significant climate change. However, it would ultimately stabilize atmospheric carbon dioxide levels and, eventually, climate change.

FIGURE 29 The World's Fossil Fuel Reserves

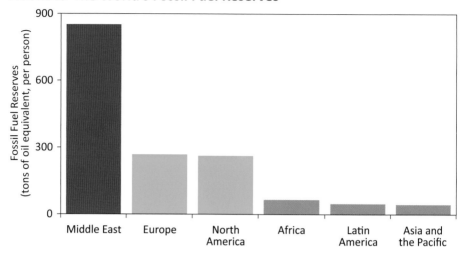

Fossil Fuel Reserves (tons of oil equivalent, per person)

Categories (x-axis): Middle East, Europe, North America, Africa, Latin America, Asia and the Pacific

On a per capita basis, the majority of the world's remaining reserves of fossil fuels lies beneath the Middle East. To ensure energy independence and greater security, industrialized nations such as the United States, as well as developing nations in Africa and Latin America, must rely on home-grown, renewable sources of energy such as hydropower, solar, and wind energy.

FIGURE 30 The Future of Energy: Home-Grown Renewables

One of the ten steps to preventing dangerous climate change is powering the state of Texas with wind energy. West Texas is well on its way to meeting this goal, as many prepare to cash in on the benefits of a switch from old-school fossil fuels to new green energy. Today, rusting oil pumps are rapidly being surrounded by forests of high-tech wind turbines, such as this wind farm operated by the Florida Power and Light Company in McCamey, Texas.

FIGURE SOURCES
(1) Photo: Milley Hawley, Kivalina, AK. (2, 3) HadCRUT3, CET, www.metoffice.gov.uk/hadobs (4) NASA GISS Surface Temperature Analysis. (5) Photo: C. Mayhew & R. Simmon (NASA/GSFC), NOAA/NGDC, DMSP Digital Archive. Map: J. VanDorn, based on NASA GISS Surface Temperature Analysis. (6) Photo: K. Hayhoe. (7) HadCRUT3; Mann & Jones (2003). (8) WRI/CAIT. (9) EDGAR V32FT2000. (10) AA Index: IAGA Bulletin 32; PMOD v.d41_61_0810: WRC, Davos, Switzerland; Temperature: HadCRUT3. (11) Keeling et al. (2008), Marland et al. (2008), Neftel et al. (2004). (12, 13) HadCRUT3, WCRP CMIP3 multi-model dataset available courtesy of the IPCC AR4/PCMDI and WCRP's WGCM. (14) Alley (2004), Lea et al. (2003), Keeling et al. (2008), Neftel et al. (2004), Petit et al. (2001), Stenni et al. (2006), Stott et al. (2004), Zhao et al. (2004). (15) Photo: Kendrick Taylor, Desert Research Institute. (16) LLNL-Reclamation-SCU downscaled climate projections, LLNL Green Data Oasis; maps by J. VanDorn. (17) Emanuel (2005). (18) NASA/JAXA. (19) Photo: Jesse Allen, NASA, based on MODIS land surface temperature data. (20) Dai et al. (2004). (21) Photos: W.C. Alden, B. Reardon, courtesy of USGS Photographic Library. (22) Photos: L. Thompson, NSICD Glacier Photograph Collection. (23) National Snow and Ice Data Center, map by D. Gerratt. (24) NASA/Goddard Space Flight Center Scientific Visualization Studio. (25) Church & White (2006), IPCC (2007). (26) SRTM30 PLUS v.2.0; map by R. Rodhe, Global Warming Art. (27) McMichael et al. (2004). (28) Marland et al. (2008), Raupach et al. (2007), Pacala & Socolow (2004). (29) WRI/CAIT. (30) Photo: copyright (c) 2009 by Joshua Wolfe. From *Climate Change: Picturing the Science* by Gavin Schmidt and Joshua Wolfe. Used by permission of W.W. Norton & Company, Inc.

The amount of carbon dioxide being absorbed by plants is also decreasing. Warmer weather, a shorter snow season, and increased patterns of drought have led to more frequent and widespread forest fires in recent years. This trend is also expected to increase in the future.

So all indications are that—if we sit back and leave it up to nature to determine the consequences of our actions—the results are likely to be more, not less, severe than we imagine today.

What We Can Expect Where We Live

How much climate will change also depends on the part of the world you're looking at. Because climate models divide the earth into tiny little boxes to generate their projections, we can also use them to study how climate change would affect different regions of the earth.

We've seen that already the Arctic has warmed about twice as fast as the rest of the world (Figure 5 in the center insert). In the future, this trend is likely to continue. Within the next two decades, the Arctic could warm by up to 4°F, while the rest of the continental United States and Canada could warm by 1–2°F.

Using advanced regional modeling and statistical techniques, scientists can also generate a host of new information on how climate change might be expected to affect us in the future—not just globally, but regionally and locally; in the places where we live and spend important portions of our lives. This research shows that, depending on where you live, you could see relatively larger or smaller changes in temperature and climate.

In the United States, for example, only the hottest parts of the Southwest currently experience more than a week or two with daytime temperatures over 100°F. Under lower emissions, average summertime temperatures in excess of 100°F could spread across much of the southern and central parts of the country before the end of this century (see Figure 16). Under higher emissions, the entire nation could experience weeks of these extreme heat days each year.

Across much of the rest of the country, increasing heat and humidity are expected to make summers hot, sticky, and oppressive. Within a generation or two, a summer in New York City could feel more like Norfolk, Virginia, does today under lower emissions. Under higher emissions, New York would feel like Atlanta. Similar changes are expected for Chicago. Under lower emissions, a Chicago summer would make you feel as if you had migrated to Atlanta. Under higher emissions, temperatures in Chicago would rise more quickly, making you feel as if you had moved to Mobile, Alabama, before the end of the century.

Looking to the Future: How Will the Earth Respond?

Both human society and the natural environment are perfectly adapted to our current climate. The consequence of this perfect adaptation that has helped us in the past is that we are remarkably ill-suited to any changes in that climate. And, in the next section, we'll explore the implications of future climate change for our world. We'll talk about past changes that have already been observed, and take a look at what is expected for the future.

part four

effects

13

INCREASING EXTREMES

"Climate change is not only increasing average temperatures, but also the frequency and severity of extreme temperature events. While any one event cannot be attributed to climate change, this heat wave [in Australia, early 2009] is certainly consistent with that expectation. In a warming world we can expect similar extreme events more often."

—Perry Wiles, Climatologist,
Australian Bureau of Meteorology

One of the first and most obvious ways that climate change is grabbing our attention is through its influence on *extremes*. All around the world, extreme hot temperature and rainfall events are becoming more common: hot days, heat waves, heavy downpours, and droughts. All of these events are consistent with what we would expect from warming temperatures. And all of these trends are only expected to get worse in the future.

What we are seeing around the world is that climate is getting more extreme. Some of the changes are positive. For example, cold extremes are becoming less frequent. And most people wouldn't miss killer frosts or a day so cold your scarf freezes to your nose.

At the other end of the spectrum, however, the hottest days are also getting hotter. The number of extreme heat days is increasing. And this is happening not just in a few locations, but around the world. Changes are largest over North America and Europe, and they are felt more in urban centers than in the country. This is because the heat is being superimposed on top of cities' existing urban heat island effect. And climate change is likely the reason.

Climate Change Extremes

It's impossible to say that one extreme event was *definitely* caused by climate change. But what we *can* say is that we have weighted the dice in favor of such events happening.

Every day we make decisions that increase the risk of something undesirable happening to us. We get in our car to drive to work, knowing there is a slight risk of being hit from behind by a driver who is trying to retrieve his cell phone from under the gas pedal. We eat a large helping of greasy food for lunch, knowing full well the consequences for our arteries. We commit to a mortgage, aware that the real estate market these days is chancy at best.

You can't be sure if you get into an accident, develop heart problems, or experience a bank foreclosure, that it was 100 percent due to the choices you made. But most of us can acknowledge that there are some things we do that increase the risk of an unusual but unfortunate thing happening to us.

In the same way, the energy choices we've made have led to warming temperatures and the climate changes that have accompanied them. These have increased the risk of many rare events. We have loaded the dice against ourselves.

Hurricanes and Heat Waves

In August 2005, Hurricane Katrina devastated New Orleans and the surrounding area. Gale-force winds pushed waves over levees, breaching the city's defenses and flooding it. Floodwaters submerged 80 percent of the city with up to fifteen feet of water in some places. All told, this hurricane is estimated to have been responsible for more than eighteen hundred deaths and more than $80 billion in damages and counting. Repairs and reconstruction continue to this day.

Did global warming cause Katrina, as some claim?

In July 2003, Europe was overwhelmed by a prolonged period of extremely high heat. Over some parts of France, temperatures at the peak of the heat wave were almost 20°F warmer than average. Even worse, the killer heat persisted day after day, with no relief at night. With a population ill prepared to cope with extreme heat, the death toll soon became overwhelming. Bodies piled up in the morgues, the flower markets, the butcher shops. Every refrigerated surface available was used to store the bodies of nearly twenty thousand dead in France and over fifty thousand more in surrounding nations.

Was this heat wave a direct result of global warming?

In early 2009, southern Australia was devastated by a series of catastrophic brush fires that wiped out entire towns, killing over two hundred people and millions of animals. Figure 19 shows how an extended period of drought combined with temperatures up to 20°F above normal to create the optimal conditions for fires.

So did climate change play a role?

Warming temperatures cannot be blamed as directly responsible for any single, extreme, rare event. However, if we dig a little deeper, we'll see that there is a valid link between long-term climate change and the frequency and severity of certain weather extremes: hurricanes, heat waves, droughts, and wildfires.

Warmer Temperatures, Stronger Storms

The 2005 hurricane season shot climate change to the top of our national awareness. We experienced the highest number of named storms on record that year. For the first time ever, the U.S. National Hurricane Center ran out of names and used Greek letters to designate the storms. The devastation of Hurricane Katrina, the worst ever on record in terms of damages, followed closely by Hurricane Rita, fueled the debate regarding whether climate change was to blame.

There is no question that the situation in New Orleans was a disaster waiting to happen. The city had expanded far beyond its original location and had removed much of the protective wetlands that absorb storm surges and protect its coast. A long history of crumbling, inadequate levees also characterized the city, fifty-three of which ruptured during the height of the storm. The U.S. Army Corps of Engineers concluded that system design flaws were primarily responsible for the levee failures. So there is no way that climate change can be blamed directly for this tragedy. On the other hand, many justifiably argue that climate change had stacked the deck in favor of a Katrina-like event. How could this be?

Anyone watching the Weather Channel when a hurricane is churning out in the Gulf of Mexico or Atlantic Ocean will see the forecasters overlay the swirling clouds over a map of colored sea surface temperatures. You can see one of these maps, for Hurricane Rita, in Figure 18. Pointing at the warmer areas, forecasters will tell you that if the storm passes over these warm pools, it may pick up enough energy to ratchet it up from a Category 1 to a Category 3 or even a Category 5 hurricane.

Hurricanes are fueled by warm water. They cannot occur when ocean surface temperatures are cooler than 80°F. Over the last few decades, ocean surface temperatures have warmed steadily, much in step with global air temperatures over that time. Much of that change can be directly attributed to human-induced warming. So what we've done is create more fuel, or food, for storms.

All else being equal, we'd expect that the storms we see would be getting stronger and maybe the season longer, because they would have more to feed on, over a longer period of time. And this is exactly what we *are* seeing. Figure 17 shows how, since the

1970s, the power of hurricanes has been increasing in step with ocean temperatures.

It is debatable whether the actual number of tropical storms and/or hurricanes has changed much. However, the number of really severe storms—Category 4 and 5 hurricanes, like Rita and Katrina—has increased. Globally, the number of major hurricanes has increased by about 75 percent since 1970.

Hurricane formation is a complicated, dynamic process, depending on the way small eddies in the trade-wind bands that wrap the tropics spin off from that flow. Scientific debates concerning the exact nature of climate change's influence on hurricanes are ongoing. In the future, it appears that climate change could result in fewer numbers of hurricanes globally, but more intense hurricanes in certain places such as the Atlantic. And stronger, fewer storms may have just as bad—quite possibly, worse—consequences than what we experience today.

Heat Waves and Wildfires

Climate change cannot be found responsible for any individual heat wave, any more than it is responsible for a specific hurricane. But once more, a connection between rising temperatures and heat waves is evident from the observations. Prolonged periods of extreme heat had certainly tortured Europeans before the killer heat wave of 2003. Scientists are able to analyze the chances of such events, based on historical records. And, in the case of the European Heat Wave of 2003, they found that climate change had doubled the risk of that event.

Globally, extreme heat days are becoming more frequent as temperatures rise. And these trends are expected to accelerate in the future. Even more alarming are the recent trends toward simultaneous heat waves *and* droughts—a one-two punch creating ideal conditions for fire outbreaks.

Several years ago, a study of wildfires in Australia concluded that climate change was likely to increase the risk of such events, particularly in the southeast part of the country. Fires were projected to become more frequent, and spread more quickly than they had before.

Fast-forward a few years to early 2009, when Australia was still immersed in its longest drought in history. Known as the "Big Dry," years of near-zero rainfall in the southeast had depleted reservoirs and streams. This decimated the agricultural community to the tune of more than $20 billion in lost harvests. Winter grain harvests were down 42 percent, rice yields were reduced by 90 percent, and livestock prices plummeted as farmers were forced to sell off their stock in the face of feed shortages.

In February 2009, this extended drought combined with a record-breaking heat wave to create the perfect conditions for devastating brush fires that ripped across Southern Australia. These fires were Australia's worst natural disaster, killing over two hundred people and leaving seven thousand more homeless.

Did climate change *cause* these fires? No, arson is suspected to have started many of these fires. But would the fires have spread so quickly and widely if it were not for the exceptionally hot, dry conditions? Very likely, not. Just as predicted, climate change may have created the ideal conditions, mountains of dry tinder just waiting for a spark to ignite.

Similar conditions are arising elsewhere in the world. More frequent and devastating forest fires in the western United States and Canada have been linked to climate-driven increases in warm weather and drought patterns.

Climate change can't be blamed for any single event. But it is stacking the weather's hand against us, increasing our risk of being dealt one of these devastating events.

14

WATER: FEAST OR FAMINE

"A third of the African population has already fallen prey to droughts, floods and resource-based conflicts resulting from global warming."

—*African Church Leaders Statement on Climate Change and Water* (2008)

"Climate change, it's happening. It's happening today and those who suffer the most are the poorest in Africa. Where there was already drought, the droughts are getting worse. Where there was already flooding the floodings are getting worse, as we speak."

—Jan Egeland, Former United Nations Undersecretary-General for Humanitarian Affairs

Temperature is not the only indicator of the unusual conditions our planet has experienced in recent years. Rainfall patterns are shifting as well. Paradoxically, it could get wetter and drier at the same time.

This is exactly what is being observed in many regions around the world. Northern latitudes, particularly the Arctic, are experiencing more rain and snow. Rainfall in the tropics is becoming more extreme, combining extended droughts with heavy downpours. Scientists now estimate that global rainfall could increase up to three times more than predicted by climate models.

In other parts of the world, it is getting drier. This is particularly true for areas in the subtropics, within thirty degrees of the equator. The subtropics are home to much of Africa and Asia's population. Droughts are always a part of life in these dry areas. But lately, these dry periods have been getting more frequent, and they are lasting longer. Figure 20 shows the hundred-year record of drought conditions in central Africa.

Studies suggest that the U.S. Southwest could soon follow suit. Home to many growing urban centers, by the end of the century the already water-challenged mountains and deserts of Arizona, Colorado, and California could descend into a near-permanent state of drought.

More frequent rains *and* droughts are just one example of how climate change can mean feast-or-famine conditions. Places that are already wet are getting even more rain, while dry areas are drying out even more. Traditional patterns of rain and drought are becoming unpredictable.

Unpredictable Rain

The timing of rainfall patterns is also shifting. The wettest days of the year, the number of days with more than an inch or two of rainfall, the intensity of rainfall: all of these are showing increases around the world, especially in tropical areas.

For some regions, this means more-frequent intense downpours that can often result in flooding. In the United States, the Northeast and the Midwest regions in particular have been experiencing more than their fair share of heavy rainfall and flooding events. If conditions are right, these downpours can trigger massive floods that can flood fields and towns for days on end.

Heavy downpours are likely to become more common across these regions. This would raise the risk of flooding. But at the same time, the frequency of drought across much of the United States is projected to increase, particularly across the already arid Southwest. So in other words, when it's already wet it is likely to get even wetter; and when it's dry, it will get drier. Again, no good news on any account.

Here in North America, most of our water comes from snow-melt, rainfall, and groundwater. Although some areas of the continent have more than enough water to meet their needs, others are already water-challenged.

Across the Great Plains, most of the water required to support the region's thriving agriculture and ranching economy comes from aquifers deep underground. Water levels in these aquifers have shrunk noticeably since irrigation began, by more than 150 feet in some places. Warmer temperatures and changing rainfall patterns will increase farmers' dependence on this potentially nonrenewable resource.

In 2007, a record drought brought the Southeast to its knees. Reservoirs were depleted, restaurants served meals on paper plates rather than wash dishes, and many states took their long-running war on water to the judicial courts. There was simply not enough water to go around. And climate change is increasing the risk of having a drought like this again.

California, with its large urban centers and flourishing agricultural economy, is perhaps most at risk.

California Water Wars

Winter snow blankets the Sierra Nevada Mountains that stretch over four hundred miles along California's eastern border. In spring, this melting snow provides half of California's water, the lifeblood running through the veins of its Central Valley farms and burgeoning coastal cities.

The Sierra Nevada mountains act as a natural reservoir of water for California. Winter snow remains frozen until warm spring temperatures begin to melt the ice. This sends a supply of freshwater downstream throughout the spring and summer months. This water is perfectly timed to turn the arid deserts of central California into the fertile farmlands that supply a third of the nation's fruits and vegetables.

Compared to when observations first began back in the 1940s, Sierra Nevada snow is melting several weeks earlier in the year. This means that stream flows are peaking earlier in the spring, leading to drier conditions throughout the rest of the spring and summer.

Why does this matter? It's still the same amount of water, isn't it? The answer to that lies in California's highly regulated water management system.

Early settlers to the Central Valley recognized quickly that water was their limiting resource. Water rights dating back generations allow certain farmers to withdraw a stated amount of water from the rivers at certain times to irrigate their crops. More recently established farms ended up with less-desirable dates and/ or smaller amounts of water. In contrast, older farms maintained their rights to the best times and the most water.

All this is changing now. Earlier and faster melt means that some of the Johnny-come-latelies may soon possess more valuable water rights than those who've been there for generations.

It isn't just the pioneer pedigree that's in dispute. As summer flows drop lower and lower, new conflicts are surfacing between urban and rural users, each of whom has been promised a certain amount of water. When promised amounts are summed up these days, they usually add up to more than the total water available for the state.

Current "water wars" may be just a minor preview of what's to come. If temperatures continue to warm, more winter precipitation will fall as rain, instantly washing down the rivers and out to sea. Less will fall as snow to be stored in the snowpack reservoir. By the end of the century, as much as 90 percent of the snowpack could be gone—and that means good-bye to nearly half of California's water supply.

Concern over potential decreases in Sierra Nevada snowpack

led California Governor Arnold Schwarzenegger to propose and sign the first mandatory greenhouse gas reduction target in the United States. In his executive order, the governor specifically listed the impacts the state hoped to avoid through reducing its emissions. Chief among these was the risk to the state's water supply.

A Feast of Water

The situation in many other nations around the world is even more perilous. More than one-sixth of the world's population depends on meltwater from glaciers or winter snowpack for their water supply. This includes over a billion people in Asia and many millions in South America.

Over the last few decades, mountain glaciers around the world have been melting faster and faster. From South America to Africa, scientists can compare old photographs of the glaciers with what they look like today. In almost every case, the glacier is much smaller now than it used to be.

It is true that warmer temperatures have caused a very small number of glaciers to increase in size. Warmer air means more snow. But if climate were not changing, we would expect roughly half of the world's glaciers to be retreating, and half to be advancing.

That is far from what we see today. Since the 1980s, nearly all of the world's one hundred thousand glaciers have been retreating. And the melt is happening faster and faster each year. In fact, the year 2006 set a new record for glacier melt. At this rate, iconic features such as the snowcapped peak of Kilimanjaro in Tanzania and the rocky crags of Glacier National Park in the United States will soon be no more. Figure 21 shows a picture of Shepard Glacier in Glacier National Park in 1913 and again, in 2005. Once home to 150 glaciers, only 27 remain today. Even these will likely be gone within the next twenty years.

As glacier melt has accelerated over the past decade and more, the amount of water flowing down the rivers to supply the fertile plains of India, the teeming millions of Bangladesh, the yellow waters of the Yangtze, and the bustling cities of South America has increased significantly. Some places are now suffering from a water overabundance. High river flows and more frequent flooding events are combining to provide an unwanted feast of water.

Down in the Indo-Gangetic Plains, water from the Gangotri Glacier supplies up to 70 percent of the Ganges flow during dry summer months. Today, this glacier is shrinking at a rate of forty yards every year, nearly twice as fast as two decades ago. The meltwater now supplies more water than people need; but they know that soon it will run out.

High in the Himalayas, these same melting glaciers are responsible for Nepalese towns and villages literally being washed away by glacial lake floods. As the glaciers melt, the water frequently pools in the valley below, creating a lake. Eventually these meltwater lakes become so full that they burst at the seam. This is usually an explosive event that sends tons of water cascading downstream, uprooting anything in its path. Trails, bridges, and structures are washed downstream in events that now happen every year or two, despite best efforts to artificially drain or dam the lakes.

Water Famine

Currently, some of the world is experiencing a water *feast*. However, the unavoidable flip side to this is the *famine*. Because the glaciers are melting much faster than they can grow, all too soon the currently abundant water supply will begin to taper off. Eventually it will dry up, because there is no more glacier left to melt. In some places, this has already begun to happen.

Glacier melt from the Chacaltaya Glacier has long provided part of the water supply for the Bolivian city of La Paz, which is home to more than two million inhabitants. From 1992 to 2005, the glacier lost 97 percent of its mass. Much of that was due to warming temperatures. What used to be the highest-altitude ski station in the world is now no more than a few patches of melting ice on the ground.

Lima, the capital city of Peru, is in an even more precarious situation. With more than eight million inhabitants, the city receives less than two inches of rain per year, in contrast to the twenty inches La Paz averages. This renders Lima entirely dependent on glacier melt for its water supply.

The Quelccaya Ice Cap, located more than eighteen thousand feet above sea level, is the largest ice-covered area in the tropics. It originally supplied the meltwater that ran through Incan irrigation canals. Today, it is the main source for Lima's drinking water.

Qori Kalis, shown in Figure 22, is the main glacier leading out of the ice cap. In 1977, the glacier was retreating at an average of twenty feet per year. By 2002, it was retreating approximately forty times faster, at over six hundred feet per year. Estimates are that it has already lost more than 30 percent of its volume and could be completely gone within a few years. In 2008, the president of Peru announced plans to begin desalination of ocean water to at least partially make up for disappearing glacial resources.

These melting glaciers don't just mean less water for cities. Many developing nations rely on meltwater for generating hydroelectric power. And today, much of our agriculture depends on irrigation from these same water sources. Irrigated croplands are much more profitable than fields that depend on rainfall. Only half of the world's rice fields are irrigated, but that half provides three-quarters of the world's rice.

The coming water famine threatens the agricultural basins of East Asia, fed by Himalayan glaciers and home to over three billion people.

Where will they go after the ice melts?

15

ON THIN ICE

"The glaciers are melting away. The sea ice is rapidly decreasing. The polar bear might soon be listed as an endangered species. The nature is changing.

"We are actually people living in the Arctic and we have to deal with the consequences of the effects on the Arctic environment caused by the climate changes. It's not just a holiday trip for us. We are living in the Arctic our whole life.

"In our Inuit language we have the same word for the weather/climate and the human mind. It says *sila*. So if you are not taking care of the climate it might mean that you are out of your mind."

—Josef Motzfeldt, Inuit,
Former Minister of Foreign Affairs
for Greenland

The Arctic is where the most significant warming has been measured over the last few decades. In some places, winter temperatures are now 7°F warmer than they were just fifty years ago. Most of us don't spend enough time in the Arctic to witness these changes firsthand. But those who live there, like the people of Kivalina, tell us that things are indeed changing—and that those changes are happening faster and faster.

Sea Ice: Gone in Summer

Arctic sea ice—the ice that forms on top of the Arctic Ocean—is disappearing. This is happening faster every year. New ice that re-forms during the winter is thinner, making it easier to melt.

It's been known for centuries that melting sea ice in the Arctic has an amplifying effect on warming temperatures. Ice reflects most of the sun's energy that hits it. In contrast, the dark ocean absorbs almost everything. As the Arctic's surface changes from bright white ice into dark blue-green ocean, more of the sun's energy is absorbed and temperatures rise even faster. Which in turn means more melting ice.

But this ice loss is now happening even faster than predicted. In September 2007, Arctic sea ice reached a record low, temporarily opening the Northwest Passage through the Arctic for the first time in recorded history. A map showing ice extent in the summer of 2007 as compared to the long-term average is shown in Figure 23. Just a decade ago, scientists were speculating that the summer Arctic might be ice-free toward the end of the twenty-first century. A few years ago, the best projections were showing an ice-free Arctic as early as 2040. Today, scientists suggest the summer Arctic will be ice-free as soon as 2015. There is no way to stop it.

There may be some benefits to an ice-free Arctic for the world's economies. For example, the Arctic might soon be open for summer shipping, greatly reducing the distances and costs of transporting goods between Asia, North America, and Europe. Ice-free waters will also open the region to offshore oil exploration and other resource extraction.

But overall, this is bad news for most of the animals that depend on or even live on the ice. This is particularly true for that iconic symbol of the Arctic: the giant polar bear.

The Bear Facts

The polar bear spends most of its life on the ice, so much so that its name in Latin means "maritime bear." From May to September, the bears return to land for a period of walking hibernation. There they fast and wander about, waiting for the ice to re-form.

Earlier in the twentieth century, polar bears were the subject of massive hunts, driving them to the verge of extinction. In 1973, an international agreement on polar bear conservation limited bear hunting. Polar bear populations slowly recovered over the last few decades.

But today, polar bears are at risk again. Climate change is limiting their access to food and making it more dangerous to try to get it. With the ice coming in later and leaving earlier each year—three weeks now, compared to just a few decades ago—the length of time polar bears can spend out on the ice catching food is decreasing rapidly.

As a result hungry bears are turning into pests in northern towns like Churchill in Manitoba. Meetings of polar bear and human are frequent enough that children are not allowed to walk to school alone. Signs are posted throughout the town: "Warning: Beware of Polar Bears on the Streets."

In desperation, young bears and females feed at the local garbage dump, where they are caught and held in "bear prison." The Churchill polar bear prison is a thirty-unit holding pen on the edge of town. Once the ice returns, the bears are released, and they return to the ice to hunt.

The outlook for the great bear is not great. A mature male polar bear can weigh over a thousand pounds. Fully grown and standing on its hind legs, a polar bear is as tall as an elephant. But the big ice bears appear less frequently now, and they're all thinner. Of the nineteen polar bear populations in the Arctic, two are in decline, and the others are showing signs of stress. Soon, many of the females could become so thin that they won't be able to reproduce. Death rates for young bears have increased by about 50 percent.

Polar bears are intrepid swimmers, typically swimming up to fifteen miles between ice floes when hunting. Lately, however, these gaps have been widening. Scientists have found dead bears floating in the water far from shore.

Polar bears' food sources are also affected by the disappearing ice. Ring seals, the most common food for polar bears, raise their young on the ice. So as the ice disappears, its other inhabitants may as well.

The Big Two: Greenland and Antarctica

The poles are also home to the world's largest ice sheets: Greenland and Antarctica. Over a mile thick in some places, the ice sheets are firmly anchored on land, not over the ocean. As such, scientists long suspected they would respond to a climate warming differently than Arctic sea ice.

In the past, for much of the year it has been too cold to snow over parts of Greenland and Antarctica. So warmer temperatures can actually mean *more* snow, as long as temperatures are still below freezing. And it's true: it has been snowing more in the interiors of Greenland and Antarctica. Snow is building up in the interior of Greenland about two inches per year, at the same time as temperatures have warmed up by about 5°F over Greenland since 1980, and about 1°F over Antarctica in the last fifty years.

Despite the increased snow deposits in the interior of Greenland and Antarctica, however, the *total* amount of ice in both places is shrinking. That's because the edges are melting. In Greenland, twice as much of the ice sheet's surface is now melting as compared to only a decade ago. In Figure 24, you can compare how much was melting in 1979, when satellite observations first began, as compared to 2007. Ice loss at the edges has been speeding up faster than snow can build up in the interior.

The Kangerdlugssuaq Glacier on the eastern coast of Greenland is one of the fastest-moving glaciers in the world. Scientists estimate that 4 percent of Greenland's ice flows through Kangerdlugssuaq on its way out into the ocean. In the 1990s, the glacier was advancing at roughly three miles per year or about forty feet per day. By 2005, its speed had nearly tripled, to about nine miles per year or just over 125 feet per day. That might not be enough to win the one-hundred-meter dash, but it is noticeable even to our eyes.

In Antarctica, snow is now melting much farther inland and at higher elevations than ever seen before. About 75 percent more ice is being lost now than just a decade ago. That doesn't even count the spectacular disintegration of enormous ice sheets such as the 1,255-square-mile Larsen B shelf in 2002, and a 160-square-mile chunk of the Wilkins Ice Shelf in 2008.

Why Do We Care?

Things are changing. And in most cases, the rate of change appears to be accelerating faster than expected.

Mountain glaciers, Greenland ice sheets, Antarctic snow and ice, and Arctic sea ice: all are melting faster than they were just a decade ago.

According to the World Glacier Monitoring Service, in 2009 average ice loss since 2000 was more than double the loss rate of the 1980s and 1990s.

It might not seem as if melting ice at the top of the world matters much. Melting Arctic sea ice doesn't affect sea level because the ice is already resting on top of the water. But melting ice from land-based ice such as mountain glaciers and the giant ice sheets of Greenland and Antarctica has a global impact because of where the water goes—into the ocean.

And sea level is responding.

16

RISING SEAS

"Such dramatic climatic changes, sea level rises and large-scale movements of millions of people across borders are a recipe for protracted, bloody conflicts and human misery."
—World Vision Australia

"In Bangladesh, it's not the middle class who will suffer the most from flooding. It's the poor fishermen who live in the coastal zones. And in Haiti, it's not the wealthy whose homes will first be wiped out by hurricanes. Again, it's the poor, whose dwellings are in the predictable paths of these storms."

—Randy Strash,
World Vision U.S. Strategy Director for Emergency Response

Some may say a rising sea level is nothing new for the planet. They say that, after the last ice age, mile-deep sheets of ice covering half of Europe and North America melted, raising sea level nearly four hundred feet. Taking the long-term view, therefore, the fact that sea level has risen by an additional ten inches over the last century—or even that it's likely to rise a few feet over this century—hardly seems alarming.

This perspective masks the real urgency of the problem. Over the past century, the sea level rise of ten inches is about ten times faster than over the last several thousand years. Not only that, but this relatively rapid sea level rise also displays a clear human fingerprint, beginning at the same time that atmospheric carbon dioxide levels and global temperatures began to increase after the Industrial Revolution.

Our buildings and infrastructure, cities and towns—all of those structures were designed specifically for what our conditions have been like over the last millennia. Before all these things were built, it didn't really matter if ocean levels went up or down by a few feet or even a few yards. If that's where you were living, you could just pick up and move. But today, many valuable structures—from airports and wastewater treatment plants to historic towns and beachside vacation homes—are located just a few feet above the ocean. In these vulnerable locations, they are increasingly at risk from even a few inches increase in sea level.

The History and Future of Our Sea Levels

Most sea level rise over the past century was due to thermal expansion, not melting ice. Warmer water takes up more space, and the ocean's temperature has been rising, just as the air temperature has. In the last ten years, however, sea level has risen twice as fast as over the last century. That's due to the increasingly widespread melting of mountain glaciers and ice sheets.

Over the coming century, the amount sea level rises will depend on how quickly the earth and the ocean warms, as well as on how fast the earth's massive ice sheets melt. Depending on these factors, as you can see in Figure 25, our sea level rise over the rest of this century may be between about seven and sixty inches. Most experts and the majority of the evidence today suggest we are likely to be closer to the upper than the lower end of that range.

What we may see in coming decades is just a tiny fraction of what we may be committing ourselves to over a much longer time frame. The last time Earth was as warm as it is expected to be before the end of this century, sea level was about twenty feet higher than today. It would take several centuries for Greenland or West Antarctica to melt entirely. However, scientists fear that sometime during this century, if we continue on our high emissions pathway, we may pass a "tipping point" beyond which their eventual meltdown becomes inevitable. If this happened, we would be committing ourselves to a sea level rise of twenty-three feet from Greenland and sixteen feet from West Antarctica alone—in addition to what is projected over this century.

Coastal Populations: Who Is Affected by Rising Tides

Sea-level rise will have profound consequences for all of us. Today, 10 percent of the world's population, nearly 650 million people, and over three thousand of our cities are located in *low elevation coastal areas* around the world. Most of these cities are in developing nations, where few resources are available to hold back the rising tides.

Coastal areas are also home to many of the world's largest megacities: New York, Miami, Tokyo, London, Mumbai. In New York, a sea level of three to four feet would mean that what used to be the "hundred-year flood" could occur once every four years. For the nation of Bangladesh, the same amount of sea level rise would be enough to flood 17 percent of the entire country. Figure 26 has a map showing coastal area at risk in Bangladesh. Millions of people would be displaced, and half its rice-farming land lost to the sea.

It's estimated that, on average, for every one person at risk from coastal flooding in industrialized nations such as the United States, there are thirty people at risk in developing countries. And in the future, this inequity is only likely to grow. By 2025, an additional nearly three billion people will live within sixty miles of a coastline. Many of these will be from poorer nations: China, India, Vietnam, Indonesia. Globally, this same sea level rise of a few feet could turn fifty-six million people into environmental refugees, costing developing nations around the world an estimated 1.3 percent of their economic productivity.

Flooding is the most obvious impact from rising sea levels. But these also bring with them more insidious and immediate impacts. Storms generate higher waves that reach farther inland, greedily tugging at whatever they can reach. Shorelines erode faster and fresh water supplies turn salty. There are places today where, already, human settlement at the edges of the ocean has become increasingly vulnerable to rising waters.

Deltas and Other Low-Lying Areas

For places at or below sea level, ocean levels even a few inches higher can spell disaster. In the Netherlands, 55 percent of its land area and 60 percent of its inhabitants are already below sea level. This is primarily due to their habit of reclaiming low-lying lands and building dikes around them. Today, these are protected by an intricate system of dikes carefully calibrated for past sea levels and wave heights. In the future, however, the nation has already determined that it will not be able to preserve all of the reclaimed land.

The United States has its own set of land reclaimed from the sea. The Sacramento–San Joaquin River Delta and Suisun Marsh is the largest estuary, or river mouth, on the west coast of North America. Covering more than a thousand square miles, the delta stretches from the San Francisco Bay nearly all the way up to the state capital of Sacramento.

Cultivation and habitation of the delta began in the late 1800s when farmers realized that they could access its rich, peaty soils for the cost of a few feet of levees to protect the area from flooding. Today, seventy islands of reclaimed land are dotted throughout the delta, protected by more than a thousand miles of levees and dams.

Many of these islands began life at or slightly above sea level, but years of cultivation have caused the organic soils to decompose. This has led to rapid subsidence, for some islands as much as two or more feet per decade.

Today, the entire delta region is below mean water level, much of it more than fifteen feet below. It is a strange experience to be standing on dry land and see a large seagoing vessel passing by above your head. Levee breaches are feared above all, because just a small hole is enough to send the water rushing in. Well over one hundred such events in the last century have caused major economic damage and loss, as well as costly repairs and pumping.

Many factors contribute to levee failure and flooding: animals burrowing through, old materials settling and decaying, the omnipresent risk of earthquakes. All of these risks can result in a sudden gush of water, massive repairs, and renewed belief that *this time*, the structure will hold.

But compounding these risks today is the fact that ten inches of sea level rise has already brought the water closer to swamping existing levees during storm events. Add another foot or two, plus some major storm waves, and it could be a recipe for disaster.

New Orleans is the most famous example of a levee-protected region, and deservedly so. Granted, the risk to human life here is much smaller; but the economic damages to farms, roads, oil and gas lines, and homes could be massive. The California Bay-Delta Authority is exploring options to divert large amounts of water away from the region and/or cut losses in certain areas by deciding ahead of time what to replace and what to leave.

Disappearing Islands

Thanks to their quick response to recent change, the Netherlands and even the Sacramento Delta may well be able to adapt to much of what is expected in coming decades. The island of Tuvalu, some five hundred miles north of Fiji in the South Pacific, has no such resources.

All ten square miles of Tuvalu, the fourth smallest country in the world, lie no more than sixteen feet above sea level and most less than that. During storms and high tides, waves frequently overtop the island, washing past houses and over main roads. Rising sea levels have just exacerbated the problem. Soon, much of the island may be uninhabitable. The government has pled with Australia and New Zealand to take in Tuvalu's eleven thousand inhabitants, but so far the governments are reluctant to open their borders to more than seventy-five of these "environmental refugees" per year.

Kivalina and other Alaskan towns find themselves in similar situations. Their costs to relocate are prohibitive, but at least the possibility is there. For Tuvalu residents, saving their home is not an option.

17

OUR FRAGILE FOOD CHAIN

"Since I arrived in Kenya, I've not met a single farmer who says they farm the same way they did 20, 30, or 40 years ago. Because of unpredictable rains, they've had to change the time of year they plant, when they harvest, and even the crops they grow."

—Richard Lough, reporting for World Vision

"The crops die. Farmers then have to plough and plant again. It is not moral for some people to go to bed with a full stomach when others go to bed with their stomach empty."

—Rosemary Mayiga,
Ugandan Catholic and Rural Economist

Climate change hasn't hurt us yet! If anything, it's just provided more 'plant food.' What's so bad about it?"

The real truth is that global warming has already cost us quite a bit. And it is likely to cost us a lot more in the future.

Agriculture is the backbone of the economy in many parts of the country. As difficult as it may be for us to imagine as we cruise the aisles of our overstuffed grocery stores, nothing is more threatening to our existence than a shortage of food.

When We Thought Carbon Dioxide Was Good

Many speak encouragingly about the benefits of increasing carbon dioxide levels in the atmosphere. These statements are based on research from the 1980s, when exciting new work suggested that crop yields could increase by up to 35 percent if carbon dioxide were to double in the atmosphere.

They were certainly right that, all else being equal, increases in carbon dioxide will make plants grow a little faster. But unfortunately, as with so many things related to climate and humans, the answer is not straightforward or simple. And all the research accumulated since that initial result has tended to qualify the original finding.

First, better experimental design revealed much smaller yield increases, about half those originally estimated. Also, plant growth in many areas is limited by the availability of nitrogen and other nutrients. Unless those are also supplied, the plants may not be able to take advantage of the additional carbon dioxide. But they will still suffer from associated climate change effects, including higher temperatures and, in some regions, longer and more frequent drought.

In a warmer environment with more carbon dioxide, plants mature faster, but build up less plant matter. So it takes more plants to get the same amount of yield. A large enough increase in temperature can even eliminate the benefits of carbon dioxide for the plant.

Finally, experiments have studied the relative effects of carbon dioxide on valuable crops as compared to common weeds. In a head-to-head match, the weeds win, hands down. Warmer conditions with high carbon dioxide levels cause weeds to grow up to three times faster than crops. This results in net crop *losses* rather than gains. Not only that, but many weeds and pests are limited by cold. As temperatures warm, these species are on the move.

The Plant That Ate the South

One of the best examples of a pest plant spreading northward in recent years is kudzu. Kudzu was first introduced to the United States by Japan in 1876 as a welcome guest. Captivated by its beautiful flowers and large, glossy leaves, gardeners began to use it as an ornamental plant and farmers fed it to their animals. During the Great Depression and the years that followed, farmers were even paid to turn over their fields to kudzu.

Unfortunately, the Southeast turned out to be the best place in the world to grow kudzu. Hot, humid summers, lots of rain, warm winters, and no natural enemies helped kudzu take over the region. Today, kudzu is a common sight when driving through most of the Southeast. Like something from a bad science fiction movie, its thick green vines smother trees, buildings, power lines, and anything else in its way. Vain attempts to keep this vine in check cost southern states an estimated half billion dollars every year, but even that is not enough.

Through laboratory experiments, scientists have determined that several consecutive years without temperatures dropping below 5°F are enough to allow kudzu to establish its extensive root system. Once its roots are established, kudzu is nearly impossible to kill, and it will regrow even following killer frosts. As temperatures have warmed, the frequency of cold winter nights below 5°F has dropped dramatically. Kudzu has responded opportunistically, spreading northward into New Jersey and central Illinois, increasing the costs associated with its control and removal. Perhaps soon it will deserve the name *The Vine That Ate the Country*!

So although agriculture might seem to benefit from climate change and more carbon dioxide, there are serious qualifications to that conclusion. And when we look at what's already happened today, we don't see a lot of planet greening going on—aside from kudzu, that is. Quite the opposite.

Rising Temperatures and Crop Impacts: Mixed Blessings

If you've been to the supermarket recently, you may have noticed that the price of food has gone up. At the same time, we've heard of crop failures, soaring prices for rice and corn, and food riots in developing countries.

On average, we spend about 13 percent of our income on food. So price increases like these don't mean we'll go hungry. But for the half of the world's population that lives on less than $2.50 a day, any change in food prices bites deep.

Half of the world's food supply comes from wheat, corn, and rice. A doubling in the prices of these staples from 2006 to 2008 sparked riots in poor nations from the Caribbean to central Africa, even leading to the overthrow of the Haitian government in 2007.

Climate change is not the main reason this has happened—as population increases worldwide, so does the demand for food. And crop failures and the resulting food scarcity have plagued humans for as long as they have depended on agriculture. But this time, many experts feel that climate change has exacerbated our current food crises.

One of the most striking ways that climate change has affected us is through its impact on global food yields. It's estimated that climate change–driven reductions in wheat, maize, and barley yields from 1981 to 2002 have already cost the world an estimated five billion dollars *per year.*

This estimate is just for major crops. Many specialty crops— such as fruits and nuts—may be even more sensitive to climate than corn or grain. A few hot days at the wrong time of the year, for example, can mean the difference between record-breaking profits and a near-total loss for the California grape industry.

Under climate change, similar patterns to what we see today are likely to continue, many occurring faster than before. New impacts may also emerge as climate becomes more variable, increasing risks to food security. Those with the most at stake are inhabitants of the developing world who rely on their crops for food and lack the resources to purchase it elsewhere.

A Positive Shift for Northern Climes

It's not all bad news. Some northern countries, such as Canada, are already benefiting from a warmer climate. In the 1950s, the United States produced 80 percent of the world's maple syrup, with Canada producing only 20 percent. Now, thanks at least in part to a warmer climate and reduced winter snow cover, the opposite is true: Canada is now producing more than 80 percent of the world's supply. A similar trend is happening with blueberries, with many of New England's blueberry operations losing out to the Canadian province of Quebec, where it used to be too cold to regularly grow blueberries just a few decades ago.

In northern regions of Russia, China, and Canada—where our staple grains like wheat, oats, and barley can be grown—agricultural areas are expected to expand northward. The number of frost days these countries are likely to experience will drop and their growing seasons will get longer. Over the short term, the economic value of these northern countries' agricultural products could increase by as much as 20 percent.

These estimates are actually nothing new. Back in the 1960s, one of the earliest climate modelers in the Soviet Union, Mikhail Budyko, concluded that if the planet were to warm by several degrees, Canada and the Soviet Union would benefit. That's because much more of their land area would become useful. In the spirit of the Cold War that prevailed during those times, Budyko recommended to the Soviet government that they burn every piece of coal they could lay their hands on. His purpose? To deliberately enhance global warming so that the rest of the world, including the United States, would suffer and the Soviet Union would benefit.

Fortunately, no one took his idea seriously enough to actually carry it through. But today, we are nonetheless well on our way down Budyko's suggested pathway. And, at least in the area of agriculture, the results are much as he predicted.

Inequity for the Developing World

Unfortunately, the story is very different for the tropics, where most of the world's population lives and our food is grown.

We tend to picture places such as India and Africa as permanently subject to sweltering heat. In reality, the people who live there and the crops they grow are perfectly adapted to the climate they've experienced over the last century. But once again, things are changing. And they are even more vulnerable to changing climate than we are.

Major crops currently grown in those regions, such as rice and groundnuts, can be affected by as little as a few hours' or days' worth of exposure to temperatures over 95°F. Rice yields can be reduced by the smallest 2°F rise in nighttime temperatures over the life of the crop.

In the tropics, extended rainless periods and droughts are expected to become longer and more frequent. This is particularly true for Southern Australia and the Mediterranean region. These droughts could alternate with brief heavy downpours that will likely do as much harm as good in terms of stress on the region's crops.

Combining the effects of drought and rising temperatures, agricultural losses averaging 5 percent are expected in the tropics. These numbers rise to a 10 to 20 percent loss for certain countries with a combined population of up to three billion people. These people have nowhere to go when the rains fail; no reservoir of savings to draw on to feed their families.

Some of the very same industrialized nations that contributed most to the climate change we are experiencing today will reap the benefits of these changes (at least in their agricultural sectors). At the same time, the poor of the world will descend further into suffering and hunger.

The poor of the world are not the only ones who lack the resources to adapt. Much of God's creation—those who also lack the voice to tell us what is happening to them, and how they are being affected—are just as vulnerable.

18

SQUIRRELS AND SEEDS

"As human beings we have failed to appreciate the intrinsic worth of ourselves, other humans, other species and future generations. We have failed to acknowledge the fact that the earth sustains life because of the harmonious balance of the elements and all the creatures within it."

—*African Church Leaders Statement on Climate Change and Water* (2008)

"When you appreciate something, you want to take care of it, and God's creation is no different."

—Restoring Eden: Christians for Environmental Stewardship

Our natural environment is already under pressure from air and water pollution, from invasive species, and from increasing human settlement that turns forests and fields into parking lots and buildings.

As temperatures warm, many of these already-stressed plants and animals have three choices. Either they must adapt to changing conditions, migrate to new locations, or fail—and die.

We are seeing all three of these responses around the world as flora and fauna respond to the increasing temperatures, melting ice and snow, and changing rainfall patterns over the last few decades.

Shifting Zones of Growth

Here in North America, one of the most common ways to identify appropriate plants for the places we live is called the *plant hardiness zone*. Printed as a multicolored map on the back of seed packets, plant hardiness zones tell gardeners what types of plants to put in their gardens and when to plant them.

The plant hardiness zone is officially calculated by the U.S. Department of Agriculture as the coldest nighttime temperature of the year. It's averaged over a relatively long period of time, twenty years or more. As such, it reflects the climate of a given location, not the day-to-day or even year-to-year weather variations.

The traditional plant hardiness zone map is dated 1990, calculated based on data from the 1970s and 1980s. In 2006, however, the National Arbor Day Foundation recalculated the map using more recent years. And what they found was surprising.

For most of the United States and southern Canada, the typical plant hardiness zone has already shifted by nearly one full zone over the last twenty years! Consider the implications. This means that many cities throughout the United States now experience the conditions of cities located a few hundred miles farther south, just decades ago. For plants, this means that Chicago now feels more like southern Illinois did just twenty-odd years ago; Atlanta, like Tallahassee; the Colorado Rockies, like New Mexico.

The growing season—the length of time between the last frost of spring and the first frost of autumn—is also getting longer. Over middle to high latitudes in the Northern Hemisphere, it has lengthened by as much as two weeks over the last fifty years. Longer growing seasons could provide more time for plants to grow and mature. But it also means that cold-limited species can now move farther north than before.

In the future as temperatures continue to rise, growing seasons will continue to lengthen and the plant hardiness zone is expected to change even more. Depending on what our future looks like, the plant hardiness zone for a given place in the United States is expected to shift by one full zone every thirty years if we continue to produce increasing amounts of greenhouse gases. Even if we reduce our emissions, the plant hardiness zone may still shift by half a zone every thirty years. In one hundred years, our world could look like a very different place if climate change continues unabated.

Repercussions

The sheer magnitude of the climate changes expected over the coming century may dramatically alter the natural environment that surrounds us.

In northern Canada and Alaska, Russia and Scandinavia, evergreen-dominated forests are expected to expand poleward into what is now tundra, as temperatures warm. In turn, the southern edge of these forests could be transformed into forests of deciduous trees, which shed their leaves every year, or even grasslands.

New England's emblematic spruce and fir could move entirely out of the region within a generation or two, even if we manage to reduce our emissions. If we don't, the iconic species—maple and birch trees, which are responsible for the region's spectacular fall colors—would disappear from all but the most northern and high-elevation parts of the region.

Over five thousand plant species are native to California. As temperatures warm, plants will move northward or up to higher elevations; but eventually those will reach the top of the mountain and have nowhere to go from there. Two-thirds of these plants could see range reductions of 80 percent or more before the end of the century. The greater and faster the climate change, the more extinctions would be expected.

None of this is good news, but at the same time there is hope.

Refuge areas can be identified. If we set these refuges aside now, many of these plants—and animals too—might be able to survive even under future climate change. This highlights the importance of planning ahead. Our success in adapting to future change will in large part depend on how prepared we are for what is to come.

Opportunists of the Animal World

We are all familiar with backyard pests who thrive under almost any circumstances. Deer, opossum, raccoons, and other urban survivors can already be spotted all the way from Florida to Canada. These guys are unlikely to be affected by global warming.

But there are other, smaller pests and disease carriers also poised to take advantage of these climate changes. Like invaders at the gate, they bide their time waiting for warmer conditions that will allow them to creep stealthily into places where cold winters used to keep them in check.

There are mosquitoes and ticks that carry diseases such as malaria, dengue, and West Nile Virus. These tiny carriers respond to changes in temperature and rainfall: flood, drought, and warmer temperatures. Some changes in where these animals are found have already been observed; many more are expected in the future.

There are insect pests that attack forests, weakening trees and making them more vulnerable to disease, fire, and death. At first, the beetles attack trees that are already weakened and dying. When their numbers increase, however, they also attack the larger, stronger trees in the forest. Given enough time (in the absence of cold winters) to build up a large population, the pine beetle can destroy entire stands of trees.

Previous outbreaks of mountain pine beetle have killed up to eighty million trees at a time. The 2007–2008 outbreak in Canada was estimated to be ten times larger than any previously recorded.

The Ministry of Forests estimates that, in just a few years, three-quarters of British Columbia's pines could be gone, destroyed by these tiny beetles that could have easily been killed off by the region's cold winters just a few decades ago.

Trapped!

For many other species, however, climate sets strong constraints on geographic range, mating and breeding habits, and even migration patterns. Not every species will be able to successfully move.

One small, unobtrusive example is Franklin's ground squirrel, currently on the endangered species lists for the states of Indiana and Illinois. A temperature-sensitive small rodent, the squirrel hibernates from September to April. As the prairies were settled, the squirrel already lost 99 percent of its habitat. Over the coming century, increasing temperatures will drive the squirrel farther north. It will have two choices: up through Michigan (where it will eventually dead-end at the Straits of Mackinac) or try to make it through Chicago and into Wisconsin. Not very good odds.

Another example from the same region is the Karner blue butterfly, which is on the federal endangered species list. This butterfly requires a very specific habitat, namely, sandy soil where lupines grow. Today, lupines are located mostly around the Great Lakes and in Wisconsin. The butterfly can't exist without lupines, so both will have to migrate together. But where? Right through Chicago again, probably.

Rather than moving, the ranges of some animals may shrink. A third example familiar to anyone who has ever hiked the Rockies is the pika, a small chipmunk-like rodent that squeaks chattily as you toil by. Today, pikas have already disappeared from one-quarter of the areas where they used to be found in the eastern Rockies. Scientists studying the pikas believe that warmer temperatures have driven them farther up the mountains.

Extinctions and Threats

These are just three small examples, but they reflect a global reality. Climate is changing worldwide. These changes have been summarized by a comprehensive study that assembled nearly twenty-nine thousand records of observed changes in plants and animals around the world. This study found that warming temperatures are driving at least 90 percent of the changes observed in insect, bird, butterfly, fish, and mammal populations over this past century.

Unhampered by urban development and land fragmentation, ocean species have been among the first to take flight in response to changing climate. Spring fish migrations are happening anywhere from a week to six weeks earlier in the year, and some fish appear to be moving north for good. These include sardines and anchovies, mainstays of the eastern Atlantic fishing industry off the coast of the United Kingdom. For others such as cod, a staple of the fishing industry off the eastern seaboard of the United States, conditions are deteriorating. Their populations, already threatened by overfishing, are further declining.

The outlook for the future is increasingly bleak.

A comprehensive assessment of climate change impacts on plant and animal species that cover one-fifth of the planet's land surface found that, even by reducing our emissions, 15 to 40 percent of those plant and animal species could face extinction by mid-century. Continuing on our current pathway of energy use and greenhouse gas production, that number jumped to 20 to 50 percent of all species worldwide.

The greatest impacts would occur in the tropics. Although projected temperature increases are smaller, species there are more sensitive. For example, coral bleaching can occur when summer water temperatures remain more than about 2°F above average for more than a month. The coral, under stress from rising surface sea temperature, expels the algae that live in it and give the coral its rich color. The coral pales, whitens, and can even die.

As much as 10 percent of coral around the world is thought to be permanently damaged. As little as another 1°F increase in surface sea temperature could increase the frequency and severity of coral reef bleaching, disrupting and eventually destroying entire ecosystems teeming with life.

The Psalms have so many verses that speak of creation's joy in the world God created. Imagine, if some had voices, what they might say now.

part five

choices

19

MOTIVATION FOR CHANGE

"The real 'inconvenient truth' is that those who contributed least to climate change will be affected the most; those who face the greatest threats will likely bear the greatest burdens and have the least capacity to cope or escape."

—John L. Carr, Secretary of the Department of Social Development and World Peace of the U.S. Conference of Catholic Bishops

"Unless decisive action is taken immediately, climate chaos will lead to increased human suffering and social upheaval condemning millions of people to hunger, disease, misery and death. Our pursuit of 'happiness and high quality of life' need not endanger other peoples, nations, communities, species and future generations that are also entitled to survival and happiness. The earth has enough resources to satisfy everyone's need, but not enough resources for anyone's greed."

—*African Church Leaders Statement on Climate Change and Water* (2008)

It is not easy or pleasant to absorb all that is happening with climate change. But if we are to make sound decisions, we need to make them based on facts, not fantasy.

Bad news is nothing we ever like to hear. But without the stark truth, we cannot make responsible decisions that can help us move forward. To use a medical analogy, it is never wise to ignore the warning signs.

Our Ailing Earth

Katharine's grandmother was a determined woman. Her mother was in the first class of women to graduate from McGill University. She followed in her footsteps, earning a degree and then raising eight children of her own. She baked her own bread; guided her children and grandchildren with a firm hand; and made sure each one, male or female, learned how to swim, knit an afghan, and provide her with a decent game of Scrabble at an early age.

Needless to say, perhaps, she was not one given to complaining. But this also meant that she was prone to ignoring warning signs.

For months she experienced sharp stomach pains, but in the tradition of her iron-spined forebearers, she dismissed them as mere "indigestion." Not until the day she collapsed and was rushed to the hospital for emergency surgery did we find out that she was riddled with cancer and had mere weeks to live. Even then she defied the odds—living more than three months to finish four sweaters and a quilt for a new grandchild and to take her daughters on retreat to say good-bye.

It's hard to say whether she'd be alive today if she'd run to the doctor at the first warning sign. But we do know that the chances would have been much better.

That is exactly what is happening to our planet. It is sending us warning signs. More and more things are changing faster and faster.

It's just that most of us haven't "been to the doctor" yet. In global terms, that means that we don't live in the places like Kivalina where changes are visible to the naked eye. We don't have regular access to the vast archives of information collected by satellites, weather stations, and scientific studies around the world. But just as a doctor would take an MRI scan of your body or test your blood for imbalances that would tell you which disease you had, climate scientists are taking the pulse of the earth and scanning it for imbalances. And they are finding many imbalances, so many that we are positive of a diagnosis now.

Yes, there is always the miraculous chance, just as there is with the human body, that God will heal the earth. We know people who, against all the odds and doctors' opinions, have been miraculously healed from a cancer that was killing them. But neither hope for a miracle, nor a small amount of uncertainty regarding the exact effects this disease will have on our bodies, should deter any of us from seeking the best medical information and treatment for a serious problem. And that's what climate change is.

Earth's symptoms are unmistakable: rising temperatures, changing patterns of rain, flood and drought, melting ice, and rising sea levels. The causes are clear: increasing levels of heat-trapping greenhouse gases in the atmosphere, put there primarily by human consumption of fossil fuels. And recent acceleration of these existing trends makes it even more urgent that all inhabitants of this planet understand exactly what is happening to it. We all need to know the doctor's diagnosis for our planet.

The reason for this is so that we can make sensible decisions that turn us, from actions that would continue to make the problem worse, to instead understanding the problem and looking for a solution.

Caring for the Poor

In the natural world of God's creation, we already see habitat loss, widespread migration, and species extinctions. Many of us have already been hit where some would say it hurts most: in the pocketbook, with stealthy costs that have crept up on us without our realizing what has caused them. We pay increasingly greater costs for food when crops unexpectedly fail; our insurance can no longer cover us in extreme events in many places; our electricity supply infrastructures, not designed for extensive, severe heat waves, collapse under the strain to keep our homes habitable.

The future outlook is even less optimistic—unless we act. Resources, such as clean air and water and an ample food supply, are already under pressure in many parts of the world. These are likely to become even scarcer because of climate change.

Many around the world, some right here in North America, are already feeling the first of its effects. Those with fewer resources and those who live in more fragile circumstances are most vulnerable. Climate change threatens their homes, their livelihoods, and even in some cases their very lives.

Rising temperatures threaten the poor, the disadvantaged, the elderly, and our children—those whose health is most affected by extreme heat events. In 2000, the World Health Organization estimated that there had already been, in that year alone, 150,000 deaths due to climate change. The estimate includes deaths as a result of extreme weather conditions that are occurring with increased frequency, changes in temperature and rainfall conditions that influence the transmission patterns for many diseases, and patterns of food production and supply.

The World Health Organization noted, as illustrated by the map shown in Figure 27, that these health risks are already concentrated in the world's poorest populations. Comparing this map with a map of cumulative carbon dioxide emissions by country since 1900 (see Figure 8) graphically demonstrates that those who have contributed the least to the problem of climate change are those who are already suffering its most severe impacts.

Warmer temperatures may be just the tip of the iceberg as far as the poor and vulnerable of the world are concerned. It is estimated that within just a few years, environmental effects directly related to climate change—rising sea levels, desertification, water shortages, and weather-induced flooding—will result in fifty million "environmental" refugees. Over the coming century, this number is likely to rise into the hundreds of millions. Climate change threatens our security, and the first to feel its effects will be those who lack the financial resources to buy it. Access to clean water, food, and safe living conditions is already a privilege, not a right, in so many parts of the world. Climate change threatens those most basic resources for life.

A Faith-Based Response

Rising sea levels, widespread droughts, and rapidly disappearing glaciers are already threatening millions with loss of water, food, and even life. In the last decade, we've witnessed an increase in the severity of natural disasters such as killer heat waves and powerful hurricanes that harm citizens of the world that God so loves. Still, many in the church continued to argue over whether climate change was really happening.

Over the last few years, however, the tide has begun to turn. Overwhelming evidence, from the melting poles to the warming tropical oceans, demonstrates the effects our actions are having on the world. Now, for many Christians, the question is not whether climate change is real, but rather: What is happening? How can we do anything about it? And why should we?

We believe the answers to these questions are straightforward. Love God, love others, and remember the poor: this was the unwavering mandate of the early church more than two thousand years ago. And this is our solidly biblical motivation for caring about climate change today. The bare-bones of the gospel is total forgiveness, freedom from any religious demands, an exchange of identity, and the gift of new life. Once gifted with these resources in Christ, we are then called to express God's love, joy, peace, patience, kindness, gentleness, and self-control toward one another. In short, we're called to clothe ourselves with Christ and allow Him to display His Life through us. And that means peoples' lives get touched in tangible ways.

The New Testament tells us to care for the poor and to be kind to strangers. Today, the poor and people who are currently "strangers" to us are most vulnerable to harm from climate-related impacts. Loving these people involves decision making in the here and now. The only sensible response to climate change is to minister to the hurting, loving our global neighbors as ourselves, just as the Good Samaritan did to the man lying in the road. We shouldn't simply look the other way or, even worse, perpetuate the idea that it's *not* really happening.

The calling of the Christian church has not changed over the last two thousand years. We are called to love others, especially the household of believers. And we're now being confronted with a very tangible way that we can do just that. In many cases, it is our own brothers and sisters in Christ who may suffer greatly from climate change. In the end, it comes down to loving real people who may be in real danger. As Paul tells us in Galatians 5:6, the only thing that really matters is "faith expressing itself through love" (NIV).

Climate change may not seem like a serious issue to many of us. But Christianity has always been about looking beyond ourselves and becoming aware of the needs around us.

But how will we do anything if we're still refusing to believe the problem even exists?

20

NO FEAR IN LIFE

> "The strictest legalist you know can fabricate an appearance of morality, but legalism will never produce love. Living under a law mentality is like being a slave to a most demanding taskmaster. There's always more to do, and you'll never do enough to please him."
>
> —Andrew Farley, *The Naked Gospel* (2009)

Seeing the effects climate change is having on our world may leave us cowering in fear or overwhelmed with guilt. But God is not the author of fear or confusion; and, as we'll see here, He does not use guilt to motivate us. That is not His intention for us as His beloved children.

At the same time, our beliefs in the sovereignty of God and His divine plan should not be used as an excuse for inaction. But why should we act as if we are free not to, and if God is in control anyway? The only way to find out is by going back to God's Word, the Bible.

The Christian Consensus

As we take a deeper look at the issues of climate change any creation care, let's start first with the points where we *do* have consensus, where most Christians would be in agreement.

In doing the research for this book, we read dozens of Christian books related to the environment. Of course, we also relied on our best resource: the Bible. If you do a similar survey (a complete list of our sources is provided at the back of this book), most thinkers in the area of Christian ethics who are concerned about the natural world gravitate toward some basic principles:

1. God created the world.
2. He put Adam and Eve in charge of the Garden of Eden.
3. He gave them dominion over all living things (and, by extension, the planet).

These biblical facts are then usually used as the basis for the following:

4. Because the earth is God's creation, we should respect it.
5. Humans are in charge of it; therefore, we as humans inherit the responsibility and are accountable to God for fulfilling the mandate given to Adam and Eve.

This is the point at which most views diverge. On the one hand, we're exhorted to be stewards of the earth out of respect for His creation. Taken to an extreme, some even propose that Christians should follow a vegan diet to ensure that we never kill another living thing.

On the other hand, others use the same passages from Genesis to assert our right to do anything we want to the earth. They claim that God's instructions to Adam give us complete dominion over the earth, to subdue it and to use it for whatever purposes we see fit. At its extremes, this subjugation includes wholesale exploitation of everything of value on the earth with no regard for future consequences.

It seems that, as a community of believers, all we can agree on at this point is that there is no agreement regarding the attitudes we should have toward what some consider one of the greatest concerns facing our world.

What Does the Bible Say?

The Bible makes it clear that the New Testament church has been called to a particular focus. That focus does not directly relate to planet care. Instead, our calling might be summed up in the following ways:

- Understanding what the death and resurrection of Jesus Christ accomplished for us personally and celebrating it for the rest of our lives.
- Communicating the incredible message of total forgiveness and new life to each other and the world at large.
- Interacting with, caring for, and building up the body of Christ, our community.
- Displaying Christ to the world, primarily through our love for God and for each other.

A majority of the New Testament writings directed at the church deal with these main concerns. According to one biblical scholar, the ten most frequently mentioned topics in the New Testament are:

1. God—His existence, nature, and attributes
2. Jesus Christ—His deity and lordship
3. The existence of other spiritual entities such as angels and demons
4. Loving God and loving each other
5. The Holy Spirit
6. God's love and care for us
7. The death and resurrection of Jesus Christ
8. Humanity's sinfulness and accountability to God
9. Salvation by faith alone
10. Christ's return

Among those issues, ecology, stewardship, or even general

responsibility for the planet is not mentioned once. We'll go out on a limb even further, though. If you were to read all the way through the New Testament, we propose that you would find *zero* mentions of Christians being instructed to care for creation.

"But wait!" you say. "There's got to be at least *one* verse. I mean, just flip open the *Green Bible*. There are hundreds of green verses in the New Testament. And I'm sure I've heard something about a verse in Romans that talks about redeeming creation. Isn't that relevant?"

There is no question that there are many verses throughout both the Old and New Testaments that mention aspects of nature and highlight God's care for them. However, the New Testament church was never given a specific mandate to care for the natural world.

Help Redeem Creation?

Let's look at the passages most frequently used to promote the idea that Christians have a moral obligation to care for the earth. The first, from Genesis, tells us:

> *God created man in His own image,*
> *in the image of God He created him;*
> *male and female He created them.*

> God blessed them and said to them, "Be fruitful and increase in number; *fill the earth, and subdue it. Rule over* the fish of the sea and the birds of the air and over every living thing that moves on the ground" (Genesis 1:27–31 NIV, *italics ours*).

If we're honest, there is really nothing here beyond *be fruitful, increase, rule over the animals, and eat anything you want.* Furthermore, if we conclude that there is an ecological mandate for today within this passage, then we must equally conclude that our mandate is to have more and more children and to increase the world's population. This would, in turn, contribute to *more* climate change and environmental issues, not diminish them.

Paul's words from Romans are also often used to promote the idea that we Christians are responsible for redeeming the earth. In Romans 8:19–23, he says:

> For the anxious longing of the creation waits eagerly for the revealing of the sons of God. For the creation was subjected to futility, not willingly, but because of Him who subjected it, *in hope that the creation itself also will be set free from its slavery* to corruption into the freedom of the glory of the children of God. *For we know that the whole creation groans and suffers the pains of childbirth together until now.* And not only this, but also we ourselves, having the first fruits of the Spirit, even we ourselves groan within ourselves, waiting eagerly for our adoption as sons, the redemption of our body (NASB, *italics ours*).

This passage clearly speaks of creation groaning, waiting eagerly to be freed from the suffering to which it has been subjected because of the choices that Adam and Eve made. But this is not a call for us to help God redeem the earth. To do so is to attempt to usurp God's role. We are not the Redeemers—He is.

Improved or Replaced?

The idea that the creation is groaning and will be set free someday stems from the Fall. At the Fall, everything physical fell. Sin, death, and imperfection entered God's originally perfect creation. Individually, we as Christians look forward to our new bodies when we arrive in heaven. At that time, our old, physical bodies will be no more, because we will live in new, heavenly bodies. As we are told in 1 Corinthians 15:35, 40, 44, 49: "But someone will say, 'How are the dead raised? And with *what kind of body* do they come?'...The glory of the heavenly is one, and the glory of the earthly is another....*If there is a natural body, there is also a spiritual body*....Just as we have borne the image of the earthy, we will also bear the image of the heavenly" (NASB, *italics ours*).

The earthly is left behind and replaced by the heavenly. This is not a preserving and improving of the old, but rather a dying of the old. When we die and go to heaven, we don't take our earthy bodies to a heavenly destination. This is an important concept to grasp—the old and the new are incompatible. The earthly and the heavenly are likewise incompatible. Redemption here is not a "fixing" but a total replacement.

This also applies to the new heaven and the new earth. There is no preservation of the old. Instead, it is destroyed by intense heat. Peter tells us,

> But the day of the Lord will come like a thief, in which the heavens will pass away with a roar and *the elements will be destroyed with intense heat, and the earth and its works will be burned up.*
> ...*The heavens will be destroyed by burning, and the elements will melt with intense heat! But according to His promise we are looking for new heavens and a new earth,* in which righteousness dwells (2 Peter 3:10, 12–13 NASB, *italics ours*).

The word *destroyed* here brings great clarity and doesn't allow much room for misunderstanding. Just as our bodies will decay and be destroyed, the earth itself will one day be destroyed. The day will come "like a thief" and "intense" heat will be involved.

It is unlikely that global warming is related in any way. Instead, it is some kind of fiery destruction brought directly from or permitted by the hand of God. It does not appear to be a slow "perco-lating" that finally leads to a "boil."

Peter is not the only one to clarify the destruction of the old earth and the creation of a new one. The apostle John's revelation also gives insight into what will take place as the old is traded for the new. "Then I saw a new heaven and *a new earth*, for the first heaven *and the first earth had passed away*, and there was no longer any sea" (Rev. 21:1 NIV, *italics ours*).

Again, the point is clear. Our current Earth will pass away to be replaced with a new Earth. There will be no improving, no restoring, no fixing of the old earth. Just destruction of it followed by a new creation. The same idea is put forth by the prophet Isaiah. "For behold, I create new heavens and *a new earth*; and *the former things will not be remembered or come to mind*" (Isa. 65:17 NASB, *italics ours*).

Global warming aside, the main point here is that we shouldn't expect God to redeem the current earth nor are we intended to "help" Him redeem it. This earth is going away permanently someday.

But for now, it's all we have. And, as we'll see next, there are better reasons to act than out of a sense of obligation to help God redeem the earth—as if He needed our help.

21

SPIRITUAL FREEDOM, WISDOM, AND COMPASSION

> "Preach the gospel at all times and when necessary, use words."
>
> —Francis of Assisi

> "Our cautious response to these issues in the face of mounting evidence may be seen by the world as uncaring, reckless and ill-informed. We can do better. To abandon these issues to the secular world is to shirk from our responsibility to be salt and light. The time for timidity regarding God's creation is no more."
>
> —*A Southern Baptist Declaration on the Environment and Climate Change* (2008)

So if our physical bodies will return to dust, and this whole world itself will later be destroyed, then why should we even bother caring about global warming? Good question.

Every day, we Christians go about the business of taking out our trash, cleaning our houses, paying our taxes, and being kind to our neighbors. We do these things because they seem right, and they line up with what Scripture teaches us about love and responsibility. They are proper. They are fitting. They are sensible actions to take.

In addition, we ourselves benefit from making these good decisions. Our living environment is more pleasant, we don't end up in prison for tax evasion, and we have a good reputation among those around us. So, both the Scriptures and the tangible benefits we enjoy support the importance of making wise choices.

Cleaning Up After Ourselves

We moved into our first home right out of graduate school. We were transitioning from being poor students to our first real jobs, so it was a do-it-yourself type of move on a shoestring budget. In fact, the only people we had to help us were a car dealer and his wife who we met while driving our loaded U-Haul around looking for a car. Although we didn't end up buying a car from them, they did become our lifelong friends.

After the move, boxes were piled up to the ceiling in our living room, dining room, and office. With the exhaustion of starting new jobs, we did get some of the basics unpacked—dishes, a set of sheets—but most of the boxes stayed where they were for days, weeks, and then months. A narrow pathway led from the front hall between six-foot-high stacks of boxes to the back of the house. Of the entire first floor of the house, only the kitchen could be truly enjoyed.

We lived this way for a long time, until we had family coming to visit. Given sufficient motivation and awareness of what our house would look like to them, we pulled ourselves together and cleaned out our entire first floor in just one day.

What a relief! At last, we had a sofa to sit on and watch television, a full set of pots and pans for the kitchen, a dining room to eat in, and an office where we could unpack our books and set up our desks. Our lives had taken a dramatic turn for the better, and all it took was motivation (in our case, mostly embarrassment at what our family would think) and much less effort than we had thought.

Similarly, once a Christian is enlightened to the facts concerning climate change and how it can and will affect certain areas of the world and certain people, it seems only sensible to take actions and make decisions that can positively change the situation.

Permissible but Not Profitable

As Andrew's book *The Naked Gospel* shows, the true Christian message is one of freedom of choice, not guilt of duty. The gospel is about living from "want to's," not from "have to's." The moment we adopt any action out of obligation, we set the wheels of human effort into motion. Then it is no longer Christ in us and Christ through us. Instead, it is merely the human-driven notions of philanthropy or activism.

God the Father measures everything we do by one criterion only: was it done in dependency on His Son? Using our God-given wisdom to comprehend the climate change issue and making decisions that we believe will help the poor and disadvantaged certainly fall within the attitude of Christ in us, Christ through us, and Christ toward others. And we believe that making these choices is a loving thing to do.

God longs for us to fully embrace the freedom of His liberating grace. Once we have done so, we begin to act not out of guilt, fear, or Christian obligation. We act from the sureness of God's affection for us, not fear of reprisal against us. We then reach His intended goal for us, a place of asking what is most sensible and profitable, and then proceeding with an attitude of dependency and delight.

"'Everything is permissible for me'—but not everything is beneficial" (1 Cor. 6:12 NIV).

No condemnation. No guilt. No religious obligation. Walking by the Spirit means acting from genuine, heartfelt *love*.

Freedom to Choose: Faith in Action

The strangest thing about a grace-based approach to life is that the end result might not look much different to an external viewer. It may not seem to be any different from a guilt- or duty-motivated life. But there is a dramatic difference on the inside. It's not a guilt motivation, but a motivation based on love, and rooted in wisdom.

There are many gray areas with regard to how Christians "should" respond to things that the Bible does not directly address. Climate change falls into that category. Therefore, like any matter, it is incumbent on us to become aware of the issues at hand and then act as our hearts and minds lead us. This is true Christian freedom in action.

If you decide you don't want to individually contribute to a solution to climate change, so be it. You are free in Christ to decide that. Conversely, if you as an individual decide to make decisions that help, that is great. You won't earn status points with God. But you will be doing something that benefits yourself and others along the way, a very tangible expression of God's love to others.

Let's explore our freedom to choose a little further.

What If...?

We *can* just let global warming happen. We are free to adopt that attitude. But we are also free to let disease reign unchecked, allow crime to happen, and permit financial disaster to occur, as well as anything else simply because we have chosen to do nothing to slow it down or prevent it. As Paul says in Galatians 5:13: "For you were called to *freedom*, brethren; only do not turn your freedom into an opportunity for the flesh, but *through love serve one another*" (NASB, *italics ours*).

Sure, we can sit on our hands and claim our freedom in Christ as we allow crime in our cities to increase and our economy to crash. Or, we can learn the causes for these problems and then treat them the best way we know how. And global warming is no different.

When we consult the Scriptures, we see instruction for living, choices to be made, and outcomes that can go either way depending on our choices. Paul continues this theme in Galatians, telling us: "Do not be deceived, God is not mocked; for whatever a man sows, this he will also reap. For the one who sows to his own flesh will from the flesh reap corruption, but the one who sows to the Spirit will from the Spirit reap eternal life" (Gal. 6:7–8 NASB). In Romans 6:21, he also asks, "Therefore what *benefit* were you then deriving from the things of which you are now ashamed? For the *outcome* of those things is death" (NASB, *italics ours*).

Obviously there are choices to be made and there are different outcomes to be experienced depending on what we choose. God makes that clear.

Doing something, anything, about climate change is a step in the direction of caring for people.

We're all free in Christ to decide if we care. It's not a guilt thing. But our hope is that knowledge plus caring will lead to action.

22

SMALL STEPS TOWARD CHANGE

> "Each of you should look not only to your own interests, but also to the interests of others."
>
> —Philippians 2:4 (NIV)

> "As an African, I urgently call on ordinary people in rich countries to act as global citizens, not as isolated consumers."
>
> —Bishop Desmond Tutu

> "Governments, businesses, churches, and individuals all have a role to play in addressing climate change—starting now."
>
> —*Climate Change: An Evangelical Call to Action*

You might think that there's not much that *you* can do personally. Maybe you picture "going green" as living in a hut and eating seeds for the rest of your life. Or maybe you've thought: *Even if I do one thing to help with this global problem, it's not enough. And If I'm going to be a slacker about this issue, I might as well go all the way, forget the problem, and just enjoy my life.*

Well, before you take the all-or-nothing approach, keep in mind that small actions *do* matter. They add up to something big. And changing *attitudes* may well be the most important change we need.

Motivated by freedom and God-given wisdom, we can arrive

at the conclusion that, although it's beyond the capacity of most of us to drop our lives into an alternate reality of ultra-green living, there *are* many small things we can do. And many of them may be easier than we think.

Before we begin looking at some personal ways we can make a difference, let's clear the air. We are *not* saying that we should try to live without energy. Energy is a good thing for all of us. Refrigerators preserve food. Transportation broadens our world. Research and development improve our quality of life. And through technology, we find new medical cures. We could go on, but do we have to? Obviously, energy is essential. But there are very different ways to get it and use it than the ways we do today.

Our Choices Matter

"Nothing I can do will make a difference. So why bother?" But if enough people take small actions, they can add up to a lot of good. In the United States, individuals and households produce 21 percent of the nation's heat-trapping gas emissions. Another 17 percent is produced by personal transportation. As individuals, that means we control more than a third of the country's greenhouse gas budget. That's a lot of power!

The good news, if you're one of the 226 million Americans or the 3 billion people worldwide who already live in a high-density urban area, is that you might already be many steps ahead. The high prices of urban housing might mean you live in a smaller house or apartment. Simple steps like walking, biking, or taking the public transit system to work or school, to the park or grocery store, are viable options much of the year in major cities. Recycling is as painless as putting out two bins instead of one at the curb when it's garbage day. Your electricity company probably offers an option for green energy that you can choose—perhaps for free or for a small surcharge.

But even if you live in small-town America with only the local behemoths to shop at and your own car to get you places, you can still do all kinds of small, medium, and larger things. And you can do them freely, not out of guilt but out of choice because they make sense and contribute to a global solution.

Full Disclosure

The dangers of taking up the mantle and preaching about climate change are obvious. The ethic of "practice what you preach" has been drummed into most of us since childhood. And we're quick to point our fingers at those who fail to live out what they publicly push on others.

You may imagine books on environmental topics like this being written at a desk carved from recycled bamboo. The author thoughtfully types on a solar-powered laptop, pausing only to itch when the hand-woven hemp shirt gets to be a little much.

This image may be true for some—we have no idea how others live. But to be perfectly honest, we do not embody that image. We ourselves are far from being the poster children for a radical new generation of energy savers.

There are many things we could do but haven't yet. They are either too inconvenient, or too expensive, or they might mean we wouldn't be able to do something that we really enjoy. Our families are thousands of miles away, so we travel frequently. We love to ski and snowboard, but it's a lot easier to take the lift up than it is to walk. And anyone who wanted to do an energy audit on our house would come away with lots of fodder for his or her report. Even with four heating zones, a programmable thermostat, and high-efficiency air-conditioning units, our home still manages to cost us several hundred dollars to cool during some months in the summer.

But there are small steps that we are taking, one at a time, that are slowly and subtly altering our lifestyle. And so far, none of those decisions has been painful. So it's time to stop feeling guilty about what we should be doing and instead think about what we *can* do.

Use Less

The easiest way to cut down on our environmental impact is to do what your grandparents told you—just *use less*. You'll save money and help the environment.

According to *Consumer Reports*, the well-known arbiter of products ranging from cars to baby products, the biggest bang for your buck is to switch out your old-style manual thermostat for a new programmable one. Total cost is less than a hundred dollars for the models typically sold at most hardware stores. If you haven't been consistent about turning your temperatures up (in the summer) or down (in the winter) by five to ten degrees when you're out of the house, a programmable thermostat could save you about two hundred dollars per year. So that's a few months to get your investment back, and after that it's pure gain.

If you have a schedule that changes from day to day the way ours does, the best kind to get is one where you can program each day separately, broken up into morning, daytime, evening, and night. Get up at 5 a.m. on Mondays and 8 a.m. on Tuesdays? No problem! Even better is a heating and cooling system that breaks up your house into different zones. That way you don't have to pay to heat (or cool) the *entire* house while you sleep in just one or a few bedrooms.

"Phantom power" from plugged-in cell phone chargers, televisions, computers, and appliances can draw as much as 10 percent of the energy from your home. One sensible thing you can do is install a master switch that turns off everything in the house except what you care about—in our case, the refrigerator, the digital video recorder, and the alarm system! Every time you leave the house, just flip the switch and voilà, no more energy drain.

There are lots of ways to use less energy with televisions and computers. First, just turn them off when you're not using them. You could save several percent of your electricity bill that way. If every business and home would just set their computers to turn off at night when they weren't being used, about thirty million dollars' worth of energy would be saved each year. That's enough to power Vermont, Massachusetts, and New Hampshire. And next time you're buying, consider an LCD or plasma television instead of an old-school rear projection model. Use a laptop instead of a desktop. All of these choices save on energy.

Change a Bulb

The next easiest thing to do is to change out your lightbulbs. It used to be that compact fluorescent bulbs (CFLs) were expensive, cast a dismal bluish industrial light, and took forever to turn on. Twenty years ago Katharine's father, driven to what extent we're not sure by the dual influence of his frugal Scotch forebears and awareness of environmental issues, replaced all the bulbs in their house with the old-school CFLs. It was the subject of, at first, a very vocal revolt. When that proved to be unsuccessful, family members subsequently engaged in quieter subterfuge. They took to sneaking traditional incandescent lightbulbs out of obscure basement fixtures and into their bedrooms and the living room. They wanted bulbs that would actually start to light up the room sooner than two minutes after you turned them on and would not make everyone in the room look as if they were due to visit the morgue very soon.

Today, however, the picture is very different. New bulbs turn on much faster and provide a warm, yellow-tinted light. Even the shortest-lived CFL bulbs are good for more than three times the lifetime of a normal incandescent bulb. Many of these last more than ten times longer than traditional bulbs. Costs have dropped by a factor of five in the last ten years, with many good options available for under three dollars per bulb.

You may have heard that CFLs contain dangerous levels of mercury. Well, they *do* contain mercury, but much less than the traditional thermometers many of us still have around the house. Plus, the mercury isn't released unless the bulb is broken, and the mercury falls out. You can recycle the bulbs at the same place where you buy them, and for thirty dollars of savings per bulb, it's worth it to save them up and take them in. Finally, powering a regular old-fashioned lightbulb with electricity from coal releases *far* more mercury directly into the air than powering one CFL or the amount of mercury in a CFL.

So small actions add up. It's hard to believe, but if every household in the United States, for example, replaced just one of its frequently used bulbs with a new CFL, the resulting reduction in electricity use would be the same as taking nearly one million cars off the road. That's a lot!

Household Choices

How we eat and shop has an environmental impact. Much of our food has all kinds of carbon emissions associated with growing and transporting it halfway around the world. Our local food bank here in town runs an organic farm that provides jobs for at-risk youth. We've signed up for their weekly fruit and vegetable shares. It doesn't just cut down on the environmental effect of the food, it tastes a lot better too!

Our grocery store offers reusable shopping bags for just ninety-nine cents, with a five-cent rebate every time you use them. The bags are stronger than the plastic or paper bags and hold more. So after just twenty trips to the grocery store, we've got a set of free bags and a permanent discount every time we go.

Bigger things we have gradually folded in as they come up in our lives. After we purchased our first home, in Indiana, we were in for a nasty surprise. We discovered that eight hundred dollars' worth of natural gas had gone into keeping temperatures inside our hundred-year-old home hovering around 65°F at best—and that was just for December.

After the first winter, we bit the bullet and replaced our old furnace. We rolled out yards of insulation in the attic. And we caulked every single crack we could find, no matter how "unhistoric" it looked. Even though we stayed in the house only another three years, we paid off that new furnace in half that time *and* enjoyed much warmer temperatures.

So now, each time we need to replace an appliance, we look for something more efficient. Our latest is one of those front-loading washers that we combine with the old-fashioned clothesline strung across our closet. (No one who's seen a west Texas dust storm would ever want to hang clothes outside.) And using warm rather than hot water for the wash shaves a few more percentage points off our electricity bill.

These decisions have made our lives more comfortable and affordable. So the question becomes: why not?

Smart Decisions on Our Big Buys

One of the largest purchases we make is our car. Although it might be tempting to run right out and buy a shiny new hybrid, there are some simple things you can do today to reduce the amount of gas you use, regardless of the type of car you have.

Keep the car well tuned, change the air filter often, and check the tire pressure. Drive a bit slower and less aggressively. Together, these steps can save you 10 percent on your energy use.

But if you are in the market for that shiny new hybrid, as of 2008, there were nineteen different types of hybrid vehicles available for sale in North America, with many more coming in 2009. These range from the small Toyota Prius that achieves an average of forty-four miles per gallon (a twelve-miles-per-gallon savings over the nearest nonhybrid conventional vehicle, the Toyota Corolla) to the mammoth Chevrolet Tahoe that manages a five-miles-per-gallon savings (at a base mileage of fourteen) or almost 40 percent gas savings relative to the standard version.

As with CFLs, many myths persist regarding hybrid or alternative-fuel vehicles. People from driving test instructors to cotton farmers have peered inside our vehicle and asked for a test drive, surprised that it "looks normal" and that we don't have to do anything to switch between battery and gas. It accelerates like a normal car and requires no more care than a similar conventional model.

Just like CFLs a decade ago, hybrids are still significantly more expensive than conventional cars. So in some cases you may be better off buying a smaller regular car than a larger, more expensive hybrid. But if you can afford to make an investment in your future, aided by state or federal tax rebates, at least half the hybrids currently on the market can pay for themselves in one to five years. And that's without assuming that gas gets any more expensive than it already is.

Where to Go for More Help

We hope you've seen how taking personal action to reduce our impact on the planet doesn't mean instant "martyrdom." Rather, concerns about climate change are highlighting our old, inefficient ways of using energy that we actually should change anyway. Taken together, the actions listed above have the potential to reduce your personal energy use—and with it, your emissions—by up to 40 percent. And none of these options require technology you can't buy today. We're talking about benefits to the pocketbook here, and perhaps also around the waistline.

Even still, this chapter is not meant to be a comprehensive list of all the things you can do. Rather, it gives a set of anecdotes based on our own lives to show the choices we can make. While there is no one-size-fits-all solution, there are a lot of things you can do tomorrow with just one quick trip to the store.

If you want more practical advice on how to reduce your personal emissions, there are some fantastic books out there. Those authors have exhaustively researched all kinds of creative ways you can improve the quality of your life and help the environment at the same time. Recognizing that none of us has a lot of free time to wade through extra prose before getting to the meat, we've given you a list of the books we found easiest to read and use in our Further Reading section.

These books are not intended to serve as laundry lists of what you must do to be a "good Christian." Rather, they are intended to inspire and encourage. As the author of *50 Simple Things You Can Do to Save the Earth* points out, it is more effective to concentrate on a few that work best for you and that you actually enjoy, rather than to try to save the world single-handedly. Remember: love, not guilt. Wisdom, not fear.

Enjoy and be creative!

23

TAKING ON THE WORLD

"When concern for economic and technological progress is not accompanied by concern for the balance of the eco-system, our earth is inevitably exposed to serious environmental damage, with consequent harm to human beings. Blatant disrespect for the environment will continue as long as the earth and its potential are seen merely as objects of immediate use and consumption, to be manipulated by an unbridled desire for profit."

—Pope John Paul II

"The growing possibility of our destroying ourselves and the world with our own neglect and excess is tragic and very real."

—Billy Graham

We hope you're getting the picture from our discussion of climate change and what to do about it that there is not one magic way we *should* or even *can* deal with this problem. Rather, it is the cumulative effect of many small efforts that add up to significant changes.

The same is true at the national and the global scale. There is no "magic button" to push that will solve this problem once and for all. Rather, it is an amalgamation of thousands of small, individual actions, coupled with our support for large-scale actions that can meet this challenge.

But how will we benefit from reducing the production of these heat-trapping gases? What damages are we avoiding in doing so? Answering these questions helps us identify effective and desirable strategies that achieve our goal of loving others.

We Don't Have the Technology We Need

Some say, "the only thing that will get us out of our fossil fuel dependence is nuclear power. But there are problems with that solution. So we'd better stick with coal, oil, and natural gas." Others claim, "dealing with the climate change problem requires tools that we just don't have yet, so there's nothing we can really do."

Neither is true.

An appealingly simple perspective on solutions to our global problem has been proposed by an engineer and an ecologist working together. They looked at a business-as-usual pathway into the future, where we would rather be in order to prevent serious consequences from climate change, and what emission reductions would move us from business-as-usual to climate safety. They divided those reductions into equal parts and went on to list *fifteen* different ways those parts could be achieved. At least ten of these will be needed if our emissions continue to grow at the same rate they did during the 1990s (see Figure 28). Each of these ways uses existing technology that must now be widely applied.

One important piece of the puzzle could be in place simply by installing efficient lighting and appliances in all buildings within the next fifty years. Not tomorrow, not even next year, but within fifty years. Another piece involves doubling the average efficiency of vehicles around the world. This is not too hard a task, since average efficiency in the United States is only half that of cars in Europe or Japan. We'd only need to choose our cars wisely—not too painful a task for most of us.

Two more pieces of the puzzle can be achieved by harnessing

enough wind energy to take care of the state of Texas and enough solar power to supply the state of New Jersey. This may sound like a lot, but if growth rates in those industries continue like today, this goal can easily be achieved. Of course, the land used would continue to be useful for other purposes too. Solar panels can be installed on roofs, and land under wind turbines can still be used for farming or ranching.

None of these proposed ideas involve outlandish measures requiring us to stop driving altogether, pull the plug on our appliances, and stop showering altogether. On the contrary, these choices will give us cleaner air and water, save us money, invigorate our national economy, free us from foreign energy dependence, address security concerns, and ensure a clean and healthy environment for our children and grandchildren.

So, with these things in mind, why not?

It Will Wreck Our Economy

Another popular argument today is that doing something about climate change will destroy our economy.

Well, let's look at the last few years. We're doing a pretty good job of destroying the economy already, aren't we?

How much more would it cost to do something about climate change and invest in our future? At worst, experts estimate it will delay economic growth by a couple of years. Instead of reaching a given level by 2050, we might reach it in 2053 instead. At the same time, doing something about climate change would involve cutting our dependence on foreign oil and getting our energy sources from inside the country instead. That money would be invested in the national economy to stimulate domestic industry. If even *one* of the near one trillion-dollar bailouts that miraculously appeared in late 2008 just in time to be handed to the mortgage brokers had been invested in developing domestic renewable energy sources instead, like wind power, fuel cells, or solar, we would be far down the path to energy independence and sustainable development. Instead we're stuck with economic conditions worse than ten years ago.

It's Antidevelopment

What about the argument that reducing our dependence on fossil fuels will reduce our quality of life? Or that it will bar developing nations access to the resources they need to develop?

It is certainly true that our way of life is predicated on cheap energy. This energy has helped provide clean water, fresh food, a greatly extended life span, and major medical advances. Our love for others cries out for the same benefits to be offered to the poor and disadvantaged of the world.

It is also true that in the past much of that energy came from fossil fuels. Hence some argue that, by definition, if we are cutting fossil fuel use then we are cutting off our access to a key resource. Some even go so far as to suggest that reducing fossil fuel use could cause more adverse effects and even deaths than continuing to rely on it as our primary energy source.

Well, let's take a look at where that energy would come from, if we continue on our current path. Are Africa and Asia sitting on enormous, untapped resources of fossil fuels that selfish Western climate change policies would prevent them from using? Is there really enough oil in Alaska to solve all our financial crises at the pump?

As you can see in Figure 29, that is not the case. On a per person basis, the vast majority of our coal, gas, and oil (converted into oil equivalent, so we can to compare them) lie beneath the Middle East. Modest resources are available in North America and Europe, while Asia, Africa, and Latin America have little to offer their growing populations. So in continuing our own addiction to fossil fuels—and encouraging developing nations to develop their own addictions—we are merely perpetuating an unbalanced economy, one that focuses on finite, external resources rather than infinitely renewable sources of homegrown energy.

We need to look for alternative sources of energy, such as the wind that is powering the new West Texas energy boom. This is illustrated by the photograph in Figure 30, which shows a rusting oil pump surrounded by a forest of new wind turbines. We also need to reduce the amount of energy that our necessities of life require to produce the same product or service. And then we need to share this information freely with those in need. This is simply common sense, not radical activism.

It's Far Too Expensive

The last frequently voiced objection to reducing our greenhouse gas emissions is that such reductions would be more expensive than just waiting and dealing with the impacts that follow. Also, not all of the effects of climate change will be negative—some may even benefit us.

It is true that the effects of climate change will not be as evenly distributed around the world as the gases that are causing it. It is also true that there can be some notable benefits from warming and associated changes. This is particularly true for northern countries, which will benefit from a much smaller number of cold-related deaths and may (temporarily) experience improved agricultural production.

However, every single study tells us that it will be a lot cheaper to do something now than to pay the price later. Even your grandmother would tell you that an ounce of prevention is worth a pound of cure. Why do we take vitamins, practice preventive medicine, engage in exercise, and eat well? For exactly the same reasons.

That's not to say we advocate an immediate and irrevocable pulling of the plug. Sudden implementation of radical standards and strict controls would threaten the prosperity of any nation. It would be naïve for any of us to suggest that we can immediately prosper while simultaneously going cold turkey on the fossil fuel addiction. We should choose our battles wisely if we want to win the war against climate change. Gradual implementation allows for industry to adapt and evolve without harming productivity or profits. But what we do know is that voluntary measures to control emissions will not work. We have already had voluntary measures in place for many years now, and these have been largely ignored.

No, It's Not

It can be argued that there have been instances where short-sighted environmentalism has stood in the way of human progress and welfare. But this is not the case now.

Today, it is our reliance on outdated technologies and energy sources that is standing in the way of long-term human progress and welfare. This is happening as we are encouraged to continue our dependence on an old, unreliable energy source that has already imposed enormous financial burdens on this country and its inhabitants.

The result is a market in which enormous resources are being invested in maintaining the status quo, just when we are faced with a significant opportunity to surge ahead in technological innovation. Yes, we are currently confronting what may very well be the most serious problem of the twenty-first century. But it is our *response* to this problem that will go down in history. Will we stand up to the challenge, or will we turn our faces to the wall when this nation has the best reason it's ever had to innovate like never before?

As Thomas Friedman argues in *Hot, Flat, and Crowded*, over the past decade the United States has transitioned from leading the way to cowering in the corner. And historically, fear and preservation have led to conservative, defensive moves that attempt to minimize damages—not brilliant offensives that achieve lofty goals.

What if ten years ago we had just stopped all our arguing about the reality of climate change and its causes and agreed that fossil fuel independence and homegrown, Made-in-America "green" energy were the way to go? What if we had started working on solutions then?

We would be in a very different situation today: greatly improved national security, a solid basis of national energy sources, and a thriving home economy, busy turning all the latest innovations into practical products right here in our own backyard.

Instead, the global market has gone one up on us. The richest man in China has made that country the largest producer of solar panels in the world. At the same time, American car manufacturers wasted millions filing legal suits against states like California and Vermont in an attempt to derail their vehicle emissions regulations.

Innovation during crisis has happened before: World War II and the oil crisis of the 1970s, for example. We did not fail then, and we should not fail now. There are things that our government can do to promote this innovation, but ultimately the solution comes down to the entrepreneurial spirit of America.

To do so, we will need to break stereotypes about the green movement. Green does not mean granola and gorp. Today, green is different. Green means new ideas, new energy, and new technology. Green has the potential for record sales and huge profits. And it will mean those things, for someone.

The only question is, for whom? Who will take the lead and gain those profits? We cannot afford to be left behind on this one.

In light of the overwhelming evidence for global-scale change, for an unprecedented human role in causing that change, and for the massive costs we have already incurred because of that change, America's unreasoned clinging to outdated arguments and misrepresented facts now comes across as a desperate attempt to imitate the ostrich. The belief that climate change will go away if we deny it hard enough is eerily reminiscent of the establishment's efforts during the early 1600s to maintain the concept that the sun, planets, and universe all revolved around the earth, at a time when every new observation proved the old model was false.

At some point, the simplest answer must be applied to the facts. The arguments denying that global warming is real, denying that humans are causing global warming, and denying that we need to do something about global warming have become so elaborately farcical that, at times, you wonder how the proponents of those ideas can maintain a straight face while propagating them.

Instead of cowering in fear, clinging to the outgrown security blanket of fossil fuel dependence, it is time to move forward with boldness, confidence, and sound judgment to build a new and better future for ourselves and for our children.

EPILOGUE

Climate will continue to change in the future because of what we've already done. We can't stop using coal and gas overnight. But the choices we make today and over the next few decades will have a radical impact on the path we travel in the future.

The good news is that, because this is a human-induced problem, we have the ability to do something about it. As today's generation, the choice is ours: Will we continue to rely exclusively on coal and oil as our primary sources of energy? Or will we take advantage of our abundant natural resources and the entrepreneurial spirit with which we have been blessed to develop innovative ways to create, store, and use energy? Together, we can look for ways that create economic opportunities here at home, ensure a clean future for our children—and, most of all, take loving care of this one-of-a-kind planet, uniquely designed for life.

Change is possible. The sounds of gospel music on Easter morning, coming from a church at the top of the world, should not be silenced by the rising waters of human error. It's never too late to act in response to this global problem. And it's both sensible and responsible to leave our children with a world full of opportunity, just like the world we care for right now. By acting today, we will leave them a better tomorrow.

God has saved us, accepted us, forgiven us, and loved us for eternity, no matter what. God has placed His love in our hearts: love for Him, love for His people, and love for His creation. We love, because He first loved us.

As Christians, we are free in Christ to reach out in love. Given His radical grace toward us, will we choose to serve one another, or will we live in a bubble of ignorance about the outside world? If decisions can be made on an everyday basis, decisions that make sense, and ensure a cleaner and better world for us, our children, and everyone else on this planet, then why not make them?

Let's use our freedom to serve one another in love.

FURTHER READING

A plethora of inspired ideas on how to reduce our emissions, improve our quality of life, and help the planet at the same time are available from:

> *Green, Greener, Greenest: A Practical Guide to Making Eco-Smart Choices a Part of Your Life* by Lori Bongiorno
> *50 Simple Steps to Save the Earth from Global Warming* by Green Patriot Working Group
> *It's Easy Being Green: A Handbook for Earth-Friendly Living* by Crissy Trask
> *Living Like Ed: A Guide to the Eco-Friendly Life* by Ed Begley Jr.
> *You Can Prevent Global Warming (and Save Money!): 51 Easy Ways* by Jeffrey Langholz and Kelly Turner

If you are looking for thoughtful, in-depth discussions and stunning illustrations of the many ways that climate change is affecting our world, try these books:

> *The Rough Guide to Climate Change: The Symptoms, the Science, the Solutions (2nd ed.)* by Robert Henson
> *Field Notes from a Catastrophe: Man, Nature, and Climate Change* by Elizabeth Kolbert
> *Earth Under Fire: How Global Warming Is Changing the World (2nd ed.)* by Gary Braasch

If you'd like to read for yourself what scientists are saying about climate change, these topics are covered exhaustively by the Intergovernmental Panel on Climate Change's Fourth Assessment Report. The Synthesis Report and the Summaries for Policymakers are particularly interesting.

All these documents are available online at www.ipcc.ch.

And if you're interested in other Christian perspectives on climate change and the environment, try:

Serve God, Save the Planet: A Christian Call to Action by J. Matthew Sleeth

Earth-Wise: A Biblical Response to Environmental Issues by Calvin DeWitt

DISCUSSION QUESTIONS

Introduction

What ideas and opinions about climate change do you bring to the table? How did your ideas and opinions take shape?

Do you anticipate that reading this book might affect your opinions about climate change a lot, some, or not at all? Why?

What's Going On?

How does the story of Kivalina affect your perspective on climate change?

As the book points out, we have thermometer-based temperature records going back several centuries. In your opinion, does this alone serve as sufficient evidence of climate change? Why or why not?

If someone were to point to a geographic location where cooling has occurred over the last few centuries, would this discount the notion of global warming in your opinion?

"Maybe evidence for global warming can simply be reduced to the urban heat island effect," some say. How would you respond to that?

How do you feel about "natural thermometer" data like tree rings and coral reefs being used as evidence of global warming? Is it reliable in your opinion?

Why is it important to factor in other "players" (not just God) when it comes to understanding how climate change can be happening despite God's sovereignty?

Causes

Why do we attribute climate change principally to carbon dioxide? Why isn't water vapor or the sun itself the main culprit?

Since cows emit methane and volcanoes emit carbon dioxide, should we be so convinced that today's man-made carbon dioxide is such a problem? Why or why not?

Based on what you've learned about climate models, do you feel they should be trusted?

Do you find the arguments supporting a human cause for climate change to be convincing? Why or why not? If not, what additional proof would you like to see?

What other ways can you think of that humans have altered our world, besides climate change?

Doubts

How are weather and climate different? Do you think climate change is responsible for individual events? Why or why not?

Some have argued that carbon dioxide isn't causing warming, it's warming that is causing the carbon dioxide levels in the atmosphere to rise. Is there a grain of truth here?

How does the whole "age of the earth" debate contribute to the study of climate change? Is the idea of a human-induced climate change compatible with a young earth?

Do you think climate change could bring "catastrophic warming and disaster"? Why or why not?

Some Christians think it's an insult to our Creator to believe that He would have created an earth that could go "out of balance." What do you think about this? And how does the Fall come into play?

Effects

Should we attribute natural disasters like hurricanes and heat waves to global warming? Why or why not?

In what ways do you think climate change might affect your life over the next few years?

How will climate change affect the poor and needy in the area where you live? What about in other countries?

What do you think will be the most severe impact from climate change in coming years, and why?

Is migration of plant and/or animal species to new regions sound evidence of "unnatural" climate change in your opinion? How does this phenomenon interact with the idea that "maybe this is just a cycle"?

Choices

Is the "Eden-Stewardship" argument sufficient in your opinion to conclude that fighting global warming is our God-given calling? Why or why not?

How do you define the gospel? Are environmental concerns part of our gospel calling? Why or why not?

Do you believe this planet will be improved or replaced? How does that factor into your view of climate change and our role in it?

What are some of the individual choices that you could consider making right now to reduce your dependence on fossil fuels and combat climate change? What are some you could make in the near future?

Of all the proposed actions that our country and other industrialized nations might take, which do you feel are most important? Most likely?

Do you agree that green technology is a huge opportunity for investors and profits to be gained? Why or why not?

SOURCES

The thoughts and facts presented in this book benefited from a number of sources.

The Science of Climate Change

Archer, David. *Global Warming: Understanding the Forecast*. Malden, MA: Blackwell, 2007.

———. *The Long Thaw*. Princeton: Princeton University Press, 2009.

Benestad, Rasmus E. *Solar Activity and Earth's Climate*. Chichester, UK: Praxis, 2006.

Broecker, Wallace S., and Robert Kunzig. *Fixing Climate: What Past Climate Changes Reveal About the Current Threat—and How to Counter It*. New York: Hill & Wang, 2008.

Drake, Frances. *Global Warming: The Science of Climate Change*. London: Hodder Arnold, 2000.

Emanuel, Kerry. *What We Know About Climate Change*. Cambridge, MA: MIT Press, 2007.

Henson, Robert. *The Rough Guide to Climate Change: The Symptoms, the Science, the Solutions*. London: Rough Guides, 2006.

Houghton, John. *Global Warming: The Complete Briefing*. Cambridge: Cambridge University Press, 2004.

Mann, Michael E., and Lee R. Kump. *Dire Predictions: Understanding Global Warming*. New York: DK Publishing, 2008.

RealClimate.org

Silver, Jerry. *Global Warming and Climate Change Demystified*. New York: McGraw Hill, 2008.

The History of Climate Change

Fagan, Brian. *The Great Warming*. New York: Bloomsbury Press, 2008.

Linden, Eugene. *The Winds of Change: Climate, Weather, and the Destruction of Civilizations*. New York: Simon & Schuster, 2006.

Ruddiman, William F. *Plows, Plagues, and Petroleum*. Princeton: Princeton University Press, 2005.

Weart, Spencer R. *The Discovery of Global Warming*. Cambridge, MA: Harvard University Press, 2003.

Climate Change Impacts and Policy

Braasch, Gary. *Earth Under Fire: How Global Warming Is Changing the World*. Berkeley: University of California Press, 2007.

Brown, Lester R. *Plan B 3.0: Mobilizing to Save Civilization*. New York: Earth Policy Institute, 2008.

Calvin, William H. *Global Fever: How to Treat Climate Change*. Chicago: University of Chicago Press, 2008.

Cherry, Lynne, and Gary Braasch. *How We Know What We Know About Our Changing Climate*. Nevada City, CA: Dawn Publications, 2008.

Cox, John D. *Climate Crash: Abrupt Climate Change and What It Means for Our Future*. Washington, DC: Joseph Henry Press, 2002.

Dessler, Andrew E., and Edward A. Parson. *The Science and Politics of Global Climate Change*. Cambridge: Cambridge University Press, 2006.

DiMento, Joseph F. C., and Pamela Doughman. *Climate Change: What It Means for Us, Our Children, and Our Grandchildren*. Cambridge, MA: MIT Press, 2007.

Dow, Kirsten, and Thomas E. Downing. *The Atlas of Climate Change*. Berkeley: University of California Press, 2007.

Flannery, Tim. *The Weather Makers: How Man Is Changing the Climate and What It Means for Life on Earth*. New York: Grove Press, 2001.

Friedman, Thomas L. *Hot, Flat, and Crowded: Why We Need a Green Revolution—And How It Can Renew America*. New York: Farrar, Straus & Giroux, 2008.

Gore, Al. *An Inconvenient Truth: The Planetary Emergency of Global Warming and What We Can Do About It*. New York: Rodale Books, 2006.

Kolbert, Elizabeth. *Field Notes from a Catastrophe: Man, Nature, and Climate Change*. New York: Bloomsbury Press, 2006.

Leggett, Jeremy. *The Carbon War: Global Warming and the End of the Oil Era*. New York: Routledge, 2001.

Monbiot, George. *Heat: How to Stop the Planet from Burning*. Cambridge, MA: South End Press, 2007.

Pearce, Fred. *With Speed and Violence: Why Scientists Fear Tipping Points in Climate Change*. Boston, MA: Beacon Press, 2007.

Speth, James Gustave. *Red Sky at Morning: America and the Crisis of the Global Environment*. New Haven, CT: Yale University Press, 2004.

Taking Action

Begley, Ed, Jr. *Living Like Ed: A Guide to the Eco-Friendly Life*. New York: Clarkson Potter, 2008.

Bongiorno, Lori. *Green, Greener, Greenest: A Practical Guide to Making Eco-Smart Choices a Part of Your Life*. New York: Perigree, 2008.

Davis, Brangien, and Katharine Wroth. *Wake Up and Smell the Planet*. Seattle, WA: Skipstone, 2007.

Deacon, Gillian. *Green for Life*. Toronto: Penguin, 2008.

DeRothschild, David. *The Live Earth Global Warming Survival Handbook*. New York: Live Earth, 2007.

Dorfman, Josh. *The Lazy Environmentalist: Your Guide to Easy, Stylish, Green Living*. New York: Stewart, Tabori & Chang, 2007.

Green Patriot Working Group. *50 Simple Steps to Save the Earth from Global Warming*. Los Angeles: Freedom Press, 2008.

Javna, John, Sophie Javna, and Jesse Javna. *50 Simple Things You Can Do to Save the Earth*. New York: Hyperion, 2008.

Langholz, Jeffrey, and Kelly Turner. *You Can Prevent Global Warming (and Save Money!)*. Kansas City, MO: Andrews McMeel, 2008.

Norton, Michael. *The Everyday Activist*. Toronto: House of Anansi Press, 2006.

Rogers, Elizabeth, and Thomas M. Kostigen. *The Green Book*. New York: Three Rivers Press, 2007.

Sleeth, Emma. *It's Not Easy Being Green*. Grand Rapids: Zondervan, 2008.

Trask, Crissy. *It's Easy Being Green*. Salt Lake City: Gibbs Smith, 2006.

Vasil, Adria. *Ecoholic*. Toronto: Random House Canada, 2007.

Climate Change for Kids

David, Laurie, and Cambria Gordon. *The Down-to-Earth Guide to Global Warming*. New York: Orchard Books, 2007.

Murphy, Glenn. *A Kid's Guide to Global Warming*. Sydney: Weldon Owen, 2008.

Woodward, John. *Eyewitness Climate Change*. New York: DK Publishing, 2008.

Social Justice and Environmental Theology

Athanasiou, Tom, and Paul Baer. *Dead Heat: Global Warming and Global Justice*. New York: Seven Stories Press, 2002.

Bouma-Prediger, Steven. *For the Beauty of the Earth: A Christian Vision for Creation Care*. Grand Rapids: Baker, 2001.

Bradley, Ian. *God Is Green: Ecology for Christians*. New York: Doubleday, 1992.

Collins, Francis S. *The Language of God: A Scientist Presents Evidence for Belief.* New York: Free Press, 2006.

Delio, Ilia, Keith Douglass Warner, and Pamela Wood. *Care for Creation.* Cincinnati: St. Anthony Messenger Press, 1999.

DeWitt, Calvin B. *Earth-Wise: A Biblical Response to Environmental Issues.* Grand Rapids: Faith Alive, 2005.

Garvey, James. *The Ethics of Climate Change: Right and Wrong in a Warming World.* London: Continuum, 2008.

Gottlieb, Roger S. *A Greener Faith: Religious Environmentalism and Our Planet's Future.* Oxford: Oxford University Press, 2006.

Harper Bibles. *The Green Bible.* New York: HarperCollins, 2008.

Hart, John. *What Are They Saying About Environmental Theology?* New York: Paulist Press, 2004.

Houghton, John. *The Search for God: Can Science Help?* Vancouver: Regent College Publishing, 2007.

Jenkins, Willis. *Ecologies of Grace.* Oxford: Oxford University Press, 2008.

McFague, Sallie. *A New Climate for Theology: God, the World, and Global Warming.* Minneapolis: Fortress Press, 2008.

McLaren, Brian D. *Everything Must Change: Jesus, Global Crises, and a Revolution of Hope.* Nashville: Thomas Nelson, 2007.

Northcott, Michael S. *A Moral Climate: The Ethics of Global Warming.* Maryknoll, NY: Orbis Books, 2007.

Scharper, Stephen Bede, and Hilary Cunningham. *The Green Bible.* New York: Lantern Books, 2002.

Sleeth, J. Matthew. *Serve God, Save the Planet: A Christian Call to Action.* White River Junction, VT: Chelsea Green, 2006.

VanDyke, Fred, David C. Mahan, Joseph K. Sheldon, and Raymond H. Brand. *Redeeming Creation: The Biblical Basis for Environmental Stewardship.* Downers Grove, IL: InterVarsity Press, 1996.

Whorton, Mark S. *Peril in Paradise.* Waynesboro, GA: Authentic Media, 2005.

Contrarian Literature

Michaels, Patrick J. *Shattered Consensus: The True State of Global Warming.* Lanham, MD: Rowman & Littlefield, 2005.

Singer, S. Fred, and Dennis T. Avery. *Unstoppable Global Warming: Every 1,500 Years.* Lanham, MD: Rowman & Littlefield, 2007.

Solomon, Lawrence. *The Deniers.* Minneapolis: Richard Vigilate Books, 2008.

Spencer, Roy W. *Climate Confusion: How Global Warming Hysteria Leads to Bad Science, Pandering Politicians, and Misguided Policies That Hurt the Poor.* New York: Encounter Books, 2008.

By Chapter
INTRODUCTION: Christians and Climate Change

Barna Group. "Born Again Christians Remain Skeptical, Divided About Global Warming." http://www.barna.org/barna-update/article/20-donorscause/95-born-again-christians-remain-skeptical-divided-about-global-warming (accessed March 5, 2009).

———. "Evangelicals Go 'Green' with Caution." http://www.barna.org/barna-update/article/13-culture/23-evangelicals-go-qgreenq-with-caution (accessed March 5, 2009).

Dunlap, Riley E., and Aaron M. McCright. "A Widening Gap: Republican and Democratic Views on Climate Change." *Environment,* September/October, 2008.

GE. "GE—Transportation Endorses New Tier 3 and 4 Emission Regulations." Press release, March 14, 2008. http://www.genewscenter.com/Content/Detail.asp?ReleaseID=3290&NewsAreaID=2&MenuSearchCategoryID.

Gingrich, Newt. "Green Conservatism: A New Way of Thinking About the Environment." Newt: Real Change Requires Real Change. October 2007. http://www.newt.org/tabid/102/articleType/ArticleView/articleId/3020/Default.aspx.

———. "Newt and Nancy Film an Ad on Climate Change." Newt: Real Change Requires Real Change. April 21, 2008. http://www.newt.org/OntheIssues/TopicGroups/tabid/108/mygroupid/7/Default.aspx.

———. "The Gingrich-Pelosi Climate Change Ad: Why I Took Part." Newt: Real Change Requires Real Change. April 22, 2008. http://www.newt.org/OntheIssues/TopicGroups/tabid/108/mygroupid/7/Default.aspx.

McCain, John. "Address to Symposium on Climate Change." Speech, June 15, 2006. http://www.mccain.senate.gov/public/index.cfm?FuseAction=PressOffice.Speeches&ContentRecord_id=D734C1B0-4F79-42F1-B7F8-40AAA31252CC.

———. "McCain Delivers Testimony to Environment and Public Works Committee Hearing on Global Warming." Press release, January 30, 2007. http://www.mccain.senate.gov/public/index.cfm?FuseAction=PressOffice.PressReleases&ContentRecord_id=3C2CF019-E9B2-40E6-AE98-4EF8EF6AA0B9.

National Academies. "Joint Science Academies' Statement: Global Response to Climate Change." June 7, 2005. http://www.nationalacademies.org/onpi/06072005.pdf.

Randall, D., and P. Schwartz. "An Abrupt Climate Change Scenario and Its Implications for United States National Security." Report presented to the

Department of Defense, October, 2003. http://www.gbn.com/articles/ pdfs/Abrupt%20Climate%20Change%20February%202004.pdf.

Southern Baptist Environment & Climate Initiative. "A Southern Baptist Declaration on the Environment and Climate Change." http://www .baptistcreationcare.org/node/1.

United States Conference of Catholic Bishops. "Global Climate Change: A Plea for Dialogue, Prudence, and the Common Good." *A Statement of the United States Conference of Catholic Bishops.* June 15, 2001. http://www.usccb.org/sdwp/international/globalclimate.shtml.

Wal-Mart. "Wal-Mart Statement Commending US-CAP Proposal." Press release, January 19, 2007. http://www.walmartstores.com/FactsNews/ NewsRoom/6220.aspx.

CHAPTER 1: *The Kivalina Story*

Alaska Committee on Senate Homeland Security and Governmental Affairs Subcommittee on Disaster Recovery. Statement of Colleen E. Swan, Tribal Administrator, Kivalina. October 11, 2007. http://hsgac .senate.gov/public/_files/TestimonySwan0.pdf.

Amstrup, Steven C., et al. "Forecasting the Range-wide Status of Polar Bears at Selected Times for the 21st Century." U.S. Geological Survey, Reston, Virginia. 2007.

Bauman, Margaret. "Kivalina Says Oil Companies to Blame for Erosion, Climate Change. " *Alaska Journal of Commerce,* March 16, 2008.

Berringer, F. "Polar Bear Is Made a Protected Species." *New York Times,* May 15, 2008. http://www.nytimes.com/2008/05/15/us/15polar.html?partner= permalink&exprod=permalink.

City of Kivalina. "Climate Change." http://www.kivalinacity.com/climate change.html.

———. Erosion. http://www.kivalinacity.com/kivalinaerosion.html.

———. http://www.kivalinacity.com/index.html.

Hinzman, Larry, et al. "Evidence and Implications of Recent Climate Change in Northern Alaska and Other Arctic Regions." *Climatic Change* 72 (2005): 251–98.

Hovelsrud, Grete K., et al. "Marine Mammal Harvests and Other Inter-actions with Humans." *Ecological Applications* 18 (2008): S135–47.

Huntington, H., et al. "The Changing Arctic: Indigenous Perspectives," in *Arctic Climate Impact Assessment* (ACIA). 2004.

Kriz, Margaret. "In a Warmer World, Alaskan Villages Melt Away." *National Journal,* September 13, 2008. http://www.nationaljournal.com/ njmagazine/nj_20080913_3555.php.

Laidre, Kristin L., et al. "Quantifying the Sensitivity of Arctic Marine Mammals to Climate-Induced Habitat Change." *Ecological Applications* 18 (2008): S97–S125.

Solberg, Erling J., et al. "Effects of Density-Dependence and Climate on the Dynamics of a Svalbard Reindeer Population." *Ecography* 24 (2001): 441–51.

Stroeve, Julienne, et al. "Arctic Sea Ice Decline: Faster Than Forecast." *Geophysical Research Letters* 34 (2007).

U.S. Army Corps of Engineers. Relocation Planning Project Master Plan, Kivalina, Alaska. 2006.

Velasquez-Manoff, Moises. "Alaska: Climate Change Frontier." *Christian Science Monitor*, August 28, 2008. http://features.csmonitor.com/ environment/2008/08/28/alaska-climate-change-frontier/.

Zarembo, Alan. "An Alaskan Village Finds Itself Losing Ground." *Los Angeles Times*, November 25, 2007. http://articles.latimes.com/2007/nov/25/ science/sci-kivalina25.

CHAPTER 2: *Our Changing Planet*

Alaska Climate Research Center. "Total Change in Mean Annual Temperature (°F), 1949–2007." http://climate.gi.alaska.edu/ClimTrends/ Change/TempChange.html (accessed February 17, 2009).

Ball, Tim, and Tom Harris, "Prepare for Cooling Not Warming," *Canada Free Press*, October 5, 2007. http://www.canadafreepress.com/index .php/article/122 (accessed February 18, 2009).

Barnett, Tim P., et al. "Human-Induced Changes in the Hydrology of the Western United States." *Science* 319:5866 (2008): 1080–83.

Borenstein, Seth. "2007's Weather Extremes: 263 All-Time High Temps Broken in U.S., Europe's Heat Waves." *Forecast Earth*, December 14, 2007. http://climate .weather.com/articles/weather121407.html (accessed February 17, 2009).

Bureau of Meteorology. "Weekly Mean Maximum Temperature Anomaly for Australia." Australian Government Bureau of Meteorology. http://www .bom.gov.au/cgi-bin/silo/temp_maps.cgi?variable=maxanom&area=nat &period=week&time=history&steps=1 (accessed February 17, 2009).

Climate Change in Australia. "Technical Report." http://www.climate changeinaustralia.gov.au/resources.php (accessed February 17, 2009).

Climate Skeptic Blog. "Measuring the Phoenix Urban Heat Island." February 21, 2008. http://www.climate-skeptic.com/2008/02/measureing-the.html.

Connolley, William Michael. "Was an Imminent Ice Age Predicted in the '70's? No." http://www.wmconnolley.org.uk/sci/iceage/ (accessed February 18, 2009).

EEA Report Impacts of Europe's Changing Climate—2008 Indicator-Based Assessment, 4 (2008).

Gelineau, Kristen, "Millions of Animals Dead in Australia Fires." Associated Press. February 11, 2009. http://www.google.com/hostednews/ap/article/ALeqM5hn9MswZT1UDQOM4JFexha4JktfeQD969INHG0 (accessed February 17, 2009).

Guide to Meteorological Instruments and Methods of Observation. Geneva: World Meteorological Organization. 2008. ftp://ftp.wmo.int/Documents/MediaPublic/ Publications/WMO8_CIMOguide/.

Howard, Luke. "The Climate of London." London: W. Phillips, 1820.

Hume, Brit. "Evidence of Global Cooling." *FoxNews*, February 28, 2008. http://www.foxnews.com/story/0,2933,333328,00.html (accessed February 18, 2009).

Knowles, Noah, Michael D. Dettinger, and Daniel R. Cayan. "Trends in Snowfall Versus Rainfall in the Western United States." *Journal of Climate* 15 (2006): 4545–59.

Lou Dobbs Tonight. "Obama's Veto Threat; Geithner Questioned on Taxes; Marcus Schrenker Manhunt; Saving Banks Again; Healthcare Rip-off." CNN transcripts. http://transcripts.cnn.com/TRANSCRIPTS/0901/13/ldt.01.html.

Magnuson, John J., et al. "Historical Trends in Lake and River Ice Cover in the Northern Hemisphere." *Science* 289:5485 (2000): 1743–46.

Met Office Hadley Centre. "Hadley Centre Central England Temperature (HadCET) Dataset." Met Office obversations. http://hadobs.metoffice.com/hadcet/ (accessed February 17, 2009).

National Climatic Data Center. "United States Climate Summary January 2009." National Environmental Satellite, Data, and Information Services. http://lwf.ncdc.noaa.gov/oa/climate/research/cag3/na.html (accessed February 17, 2009).

Parker, D. E., T. P. Legg, and C. K. Folland. "A New Daily Central England Temperature Series, 1772–1991." *International Journal of Climatology* 12 (1992): 317–42.

Parmesan, Camille, and Hector Galbraith. "Observed Impacts of Global Climate Change in the U.S." Pew Center on Global Climate Change. http://www.pewclimate.org/global-warming-in-depth/all_reports/observedimpacts (accessed February 17, 2009).

Peterson, T. C. "Assessment of Urban Versus Rural in Situ Surface Temperatures in the Contiguous United States: No Difference Found." *Journal of Climate* 16 (2003): 2941–59.

RedOrbit. "Australia's Deadly Wildfires Attributed to Climate Change."

February 9, 2009. http://www.redorbit.com/news/science/1636193/australias_deadly_wildfires_attributed_to_climate_change/index.html (accessed February 17, 2009).

Robine, Jean-Marie. "Death Toll Exceeded 70,000 in Europe During the Summer of 2003." *Académie des Sciences* 2007.

Rocky Mountain Climate Organization. "West Heating up Faster Than Rest of United States." http://www.rockymountainclimate.org/website%20pictures/ReleaseHotterDrier.pdf (accessed February 17, 2009).

Schmidt, G. A. "Spurious Correlations Between Recent Warming and Indices of Local Economic Activity." *International Journal of Climatology* (2009: forthcoming).

Schmidt, Gavin. "CNN Is Spun Right Round, Baby, Right Round." RealClimate: Climate Science from Climate Scientists. January 14, 2009. http://www.realclimate.org/index.php/archives/2009/01/cnn-is-spun-right-round-baby-right-round/langswitch_lang/sp.

Stewart, Iris T., Daniel R. Cayan, and Michael D. Dettinger. "Changes Toward Earlier Streamflow Timing Across Western North America." *Journal of Climate* 18 (2005): 1136–55.

Stott, Peter A., D. A. Stone, and M. R. Allen. "Human Contribution to the European Heatwave of 2003." *Nature* 432 (2004): 610–14.

Takver. "Climate Change Contributes to Catastrophic Australian Bushfires." Sydney Indymedia, February 8, 2009. http://www.indybay.org/newsitems/2009/02/08/18568890.php (accessed February 17, 2009).

Taylor, James M. "Global Cooling Continues." *Environment & Climate News*, March 1, 2009. http://www.heartland.org/publications/environment%20climate/article/24739/Global_Cooling_Continues.html (accessed February 17, 2009).

Taylor, Rob. "Drought in Australia Food Bowl Continues." Reuters. February 3, 2009. http://www.reuters.com/article/environmentNews/idUSTRE5127CY20090203 (accessed February 17, 2009).

Weart, Spencer. "The Modern Temperature Trend." *The Discovery of Global Warming*, June 2008. American Institute of Physics. http://www.aip.org/history/climate/20ctrend.htm.

World Development Movement. "Desmond Tutu on Climate Change." http://www.youtube.com/watch?v=onSHD4sAuB4 (accessed March 5, 2009).

CHAPTER 3. *Indicators of Change*

Aono Y., and K. Kazui. "Phenological Data Series of Cherry Tree Flowering in Kyoto, Japan, and Its Application to Reconstruction of Springtime Temperatures Since the 9th Century." *International Journal of Climatology* 28 (2007): 905–14.

Aono Y., and Y. Omoto. "Estimation of Temperature at Kyoto Since the 11th Century Using Flowering Data of Cherry Trees in Old Documents." *Journal of Agricultural Meteorology* 49 (1994): 263–72.

Beck, Coby. "How to Talk to a Climate Skeptic: 'Greenland Used to Be Green.'" *Grist: Environmental News & Commentary*, December 16, 2006. http://www.gristmill.grist.org/story/2006/12/13/22437/993.

Chuine, Isabelle, et al. "Historical Phenology: Grape Ripening as a Past Climate Indicator." *Nature* 434 (2004): 289–90.

Diamond, Jared. "The History of Norway," *Collapse*, 261, Summary at http://www.iupui.edu/~geni/documents/Vikings_in_Greenland-An_Overview.doc, IUPUI: Indiana University Purdue University Indianapolis.

Feng, Xiahong, and Samuel Epstein. "Climatic Implications of an 8000-Year Hydrogen Isotope Time Series from Bristlecone Pine Trees." *Science* 265:5175 (1994): 1079–81.

Ferguson, C.W. "Bristlecone Pine: Science and Esthetics: A 7100-year Tree-Ring Chronology Aids Scientists; Old Trees Draw Visitors to California Mountains." *Science* 159:3817 (1968): 839–46.

Fisk, Charles. "The First Fifty Years of Recorded Weather History in Minnesota (1820–1869): A Year-by-Year Narrative Account." AT&T Personal Webpage. http://www.home.att.net/~station_climo/purpose.htm.

Friedrich, Michael, et al. "The 12,460-year Hohenheim Oak and Pine Tree-Ring Chronology from Central Europe—A Unique Annual Record for Radiocarbon Calibration and Paleoenvironment Reconstructions." *Radiocarbon* 46:3 (2004): 1111–22.

Hughes, M., and H. F. Diaz. "Was There a 'Medieval Warm Period'?" *Climatic Change* 26 (1994): 109–42.

IPCC. *Climate Change 2007: The Physical Science Basis Contribution of Working Group I to the Fourth Assessment Report of the Intergovernmental Panel on Climate Change*, edited by S. Solomon et al. Cambridge: Cambridge University Press. 2007.

Lindgrén, S., and J. Neumann. "The Cold and Wet Year 1695—A Contemporary German Account." *Climatic Change* 3:2 (1981): 173–87.

Magnuson, John J. "Historical Trends in Lake and River Ice Cover in the Northern Hemisphere." *Science* 289 (2000): 1743–46.

Meteorology @ West Moors. "Historical Weather Events." Booty Web Site. http://www.booty.org.uk/booty.weather/climate/wxevents.htm.

Metter, Holly. "Records Dating Back to Thoreau Show Some Sharp Shifts in Plant Flowering Near Walden Pond: Effects of Climate Change

Vary Greatly Across Plant Families." Harvard Science. http://www
.harvardscience.harvard.edu/environments/articles/records-dating-
back-thoreau-show-some-sharp-shifts-plant-flowering-near-walden
(accessed February 17, 2009).

Miller-Rushing, A. J., and R. B. Primack. "Global Warming and Flowering
Times in Thoreau's Concord: A Community Perspective." *Ecology* 89:2
(2008): 332–41.

National Academies Press. "Surface Temperature Reconstructions for the
Last 2,000 Years." Full Report. National Research Council. http://
www.nap.edu/catalog.php?record_id=11676#toc.

National Academies Report: Advisers to the Nation on Science, Engineer-
ing, and Medicine. June 22, 2006. http://www8.nationalacademies
.org/onpinews/newsitem.aspx?RecordID=11676.

Primack, R., and H. Higuchi. "Climate Change and Cherry Tree Blossom
Festivals in Japan." *Arnoldia* 65 (2007): 14–22.

RealClimate: Climate Science from Climate Scientists. "Medieval Warmth
and English Wine." July 12, 2006. http://www.realclimate.org/index
.php/archives/2006/07/medieval-warmth-and-english-wine/.

Schmidt, Burghart, and Wolfgang Gruhle. "Similarities Between Tree-Ring
Chronologies in Germany and Nepal: An Analysis of Long-Term Fluc-
tuations." DendroLabor. http://www.wsl.ch/staff/felix.kaiser/PDFs/
Friedrich_Dendro_RC04%20.pdf.

Segarin, R., and F. Micheli. "Climate Change in Non-traditional Data
Sets." *Science* 294 (2001): 811.

Soon, Willie, and Sallie Baliunas. "Proxy Climatic and Environmental
Changes of the Past 1000 Years." *Climate Research* 23 (2003): 89–110.

Varley, Paul. *Japanese Culture.* Honolulu: University of Hawaii Press, 2000.

Zhang, Qiang, Marco Gemmer, and Jiaqi Chen. "Climate Changes and
Flood/Drought Risk in the Yangtze Delta, China, During the Past Millennium." *Quaternary Studies in Korea* (2008): 62–69.

Zhong, Wei, et al. "Historical Climate Changes in Southern Xinjiang."
Institute of Geographic Sciences and Natural Resources Research, CAS.
http://www.igsnrr.ac.cn/menu9/book5.jsp?id=453.

CHAPTER 4. *Decisions and Consequences*

Adam, David. "I Underestimated the Threat, Says Stern." *Guardian*, April
18, 2008, Environment section. http://www.guardian.co.uk/environment/
2008/apr/18/climatechange.carbonemissions.

Burke, Eleanor J., Simon J. Brown, and Nikolaos Christidis. "Modeling the
Recent Evolution of Global Drought and Projections for the Twenty-first

Century with the Hadley Centre Climate Model." *Journal of Hydrometeorology* 7:5 (2006): 1113–25.

Cook, Kerry H., and Edward K. Vizy. "Effects of Twenty-First-Century Climate Change on the Amazon Rain Forest." *Journal of Climate* 21:3 (2008): 542–60.

Cox, P. M., et al. "Amazonian Forest Dieback Under Climate-Carbon Cycle Projections for the 21st Century." *Theoretical and Applied Climatology* 78 (2004): 137–56.

Hansen, James E. "Is There Still Time to Avoid 'Dangerous Anthropogenic Interference' with Global Climate?" Presentation at the American Geophysical Union, San Francisco, CA, December 6, 2005.

IPCC. "Summary for Policymakers." In *Climate Change 2007: Mitigation. Contribution of Working Group III to the Fourth Assessment Report of the Intergovernmental Panel on Climate Change*, edited by B. Metz et al. Cambridge: Cambridge University Press, 2007.

Laurence, William F., and G. Bruce Williamson. "Positive Feedbacks among Forest Fragmentation, Drought, and Climate Change in the Amazon." *Conservation Biology* 15:5 (2002): 1529–35.

Malhi, Yadvinder, et al. "Climate Change, Deforestation, and the Fate of the Amazon." *Science* 319:5860 (2008): 169–72.

Mayhew, Peter J., Gareth B. Jenkins, and Timothy G. Benton. "A Long-Term Association Between Global Temperature and Biodiversity, Origination and Extinction in the Fossil Record." *Biological Sciences* 275:1630 (2008): 47–53.

Meehl, G. A., et al. "Global Climate Projections." In *Climate Change 2007: The Physical Science Basis. Contribution of Working Group I to the Fourth Assessment Report of the Intergovernmental Panel on Climate Change*, edited by S. Solomon et al. Cambridge: Cambridge University Press, 2007.

Overpeck, Jonathan T., et al. "Paleoclimatic Evidence for Future Ice-Sheet Instability and Rapid Sea-Level Rise." *Science* 311:5768 (2006): 1747–50.

Pachauri, R. K., and A. Reisinger. *Climate Change 2007: Synthesis Report. Contribution of Working Groups I, II and III to the Fourth Assessment Report of the Intergovernmental Panel on Climate Change.* Geneva: IPCC, 2007.

Parry, M. L., et al. "Summary for Policymakers." In *Climate Change 2007: Impacts, Adaptation and Vulnerability. Contribution of Working Group II to the Fourth Assessment Report of the Intergovernmental Panel on Climate Change.* Cambridge: Cambridge University Press, 2007.

Ruth, Matthias, Dana Coelho, and Daria Karetnikov. "The Economic

Impacts of Climate Change and the Costs of Inaction." College Park: University of Maryland, 2007.

Southern Baptist Environment & Climate Initiative. "A Southern Baptist Declaration on the Environment and Climate Change." http://www .baptistcreationcare.org/node/1 (accessed March 5, 2009).

Stern Review. "The Economics of Climate Change." Stern Review Report. http://news.bbc.co.uk/1/shared/bsp/hi/pdfs/30_10_06_exec_sum.pdf.

Thomas, C., et al. "Extinction Risk from Climate Change." *Nature* 427 (2004): 145–48.

UnHabitat. "State of the World's Cities 2008/2009—Harmonious Cities." UnHabitat. http://www.unhabitat.org/content.asp?cid=5964&catid=7 &typeid=46&subMenuId=0.

CHAPTER 5. God's Gift: The Earth

Bousquet, P., et al. "Contribution of Anthropogenic and Natural Sources to Atmospheric Methane Variability." *Nature* 43:28 (2006): 439–43.

Canadell, Joseph G., et al. "Contributions to Accelerating Atmospheric CO_2 Growth from Economic Activity, Carbon Intensity, and Efficiency of Natural Sinks." *Proceedings of the National Academy of Sciences of the United States of America*, 104:47 (2007): 18866–70.

Climate Analysis Indicators Tool (CAIT) version 3.0. Washington, DC: World Resources Institute, 2005. Available at http://cait.wri.org.

Denman, K.L., et al. "Couplings Between Changes in the Climate System and Biogeochemistry." In *Climate Change 2007: The Physical Science Basis. Contribution of Working Group I to the Fourth Assessment Report of the Intergovernmental Panel on Climate Change*, edited by S. Solomon et al. Cambridge: Cambridge University Press, 2007.

Dore, John E., Roger Lukas, Daniel W. Sadler, and David M. Karl. "Climate-Driven Changes to the Atmospheric CO_2 Sink in the Subtropical North Pacific Ocean." *Nature*, 424 (2003): 754–57.

Forster, P., et al. "Changes in Atmospheric Constituents and in Radiative Forcing." In *Climate Change 2007: The Physical Science Basis. Contribution of Working Group I to the Fourth Assessment Report of the Intergovernmental Panel on Climate Change* edited by S. Solomon et al. Cambridge: Cambridge University Press, 2007.

Illyn, Peter. "Love—What Kind of Christian Should Care About Global Warming? Every Kind." *Restoring Eden.* 2006.

Janzen, R. L., et al. "Better Farming, Better Air: A Scientific Analysis of Farming Practice and Greenhouse Gases in Canada." *Agriculture and Agri-food Canada*, March 2008, 53.

Marland, G., T. A. Boden, and R. J. Andres. "Global, Regional, and National Fossil Fuel CO_2 Emissions." In *Trends: A Compendium of Data on Global Change*. Carbon Dioxide Information Analysis Center, Oak Ridge National Laboratory, U.S. Department of Energy, Oak Ridge, Tenn. Available online at: http://cdiac.ornl.gov/trends/emis/overview.html 2005.

Raupach, Michael R., et al. "Global and Regional Drivers of Accelerating CO_2 Emissions." *Proceedings of the National Academy of Sciences of the United States of America,* 104:24 (2007): 10288–93.

Real Climate Blog. "Water Vapour: Feedback or Forcing?" April 6, 2005. http://www.realclimate.org/index.php?p=142 Real Climate: Climate Science from Climate Scientists.

Rigby, M., et al. "Renewed Growth of Atmospheric Methane." *Geophysical Research Letters* 35 (2008): L22805.

Vuuren, Detlef P. van, and Brian C. O'Neill. "The Consistency of IPCC's SRES Scenarios to 1990–2000 Trends and Recent Projections." *Climatic Change* 75:1–2 (2006): 9–46.

Wuebbles, D. J., and K. Hayhoe. "Atmospheric Methane and Global Change." *Earth Science Reviews* 57:3 (2002): 177–210.

CHAPTER 6. *The Natural Suspects*

Ammann, Caspar M., et al. "Solar Influence on Climate During the Past Millennium: Results from Transient Simulations with the NCAR Climate System Model." *Proceedings of the National Academy of Science* 104:10 (2007): 3713–18.

Dutton, E. G., and J. R. Christy. "Solar Radiative Forcing at Selected Locations and Evidence for Global Lower Tropospheric Cooling Following the Eruptions of El Chichón and Pinatubo." *Geophysical Research Letters* 19:23 (1992): 2313–16.

Evangelical Youth Climate Initiative. "Cooling Our Future: A Declaration by Young Evangelicals on Climate Change." http://www.restoringeden.org/campaigns/GlobalWarming/EYCItext/view (accessed March 5, 2009).

Hansen, J., A. Lacis, R. Ruedy, and M. Sato. "Potential Climate Impact of Mount Pinatubo Eruption." *Geophysical Research Letters* 19:2 (1992): 215–18.

Leavitt, Steven W. "Annual Volcanic Carbon Dioxide Emission: An Estimate From Eruption Chronologies." *Environmental Geology* 4:1 (2006): 15–21.

Lessons Learned from the 1997–1998 El Nino. UNEP/NCAR/UNU/WMO/ISDR Assessment. http://www.reliefweb.int/library/documents/elnino.pdf.

Lockwood, Mike, and Claus Fröhlich. "Recent Oppositely Directed Trends in Solar Climate Forcings and the Global Mean Surface Air Temperature." *Proceedings of the Royal Society* 463:2086 (2007): 2447–60.

McCormick, M. Patrick, Larry W. Thomason, and Charles R. Trepte. "Atmospheric Effects of the Mt Pinatubo Eruption." *Nature* 373 (1995): 399–404.

Oppenheimer, Clive. "Climatic, Environmental and Human Consequences of the Largest Known Historic Eruption: Tambora Volcano (Indonesia) 1815." *Progress in Physical Geography* 27:2 (2003): 230–59.

Rigor, Ignatius G., John M. Wallace, and Roger L. Colony. "Response of Sea Ice to the Arctic Oscillation." *Journal of Climate* 15:18 (2002): 2648–63.

Shindell, Drew. "The Sun's Chilly Impact on Earth." Earth Observatory. December 6, 2001.

Space Weather Prediction Center. "Solar Cycle Progression." NOAA. http://www.swpc.noaa.gov/SolarCycle/ (accessed February 18, 2009).

Sponberg, Kelly. "Weathering a Storm of Global Statistics." *Nature* 400:13 (July 1, 1999). http://www.nature.com/nature/journal/v400/n6739/full/400013a0.html.

Swiss Re. "El Niño 1997/98: On the phenomenon's trail." Zurich, Switzerland: Swiss Reinsurance, 1999. 8 pp. http://www.swissre.com/.

U.S. Geological Survey. "El Niño Sea-Level Rise Wreaks Havoc in California's San Francisco Bay Region." USGS. http://pubs.usgs.gov/fs/1999/fs175-99/ (accessed February 18, 2009).

Wang, Jia, and Moto Ikeda. "Arctic Oscillation and Arctic Sea Ice Oscillation." *Geophysical Research Letters* 27:9 (2000): 1287–90.

Williams, Stanley N., Stephen J. Schaefer, Marta Lucia Calvache, and Dina Lopez. "Global Carbon Dioxide Emission to the Atmosphere by Volcanoes." *Geochimica et Cosmochimica Acta* 56:4 (1992): 1765–70.

CHAPTER 7. The Human Fingerprint

IPCC. *Climate Change 2007: Synthesis Report. Contribution of Working Groups I, II and III to the Fourth Assessment Report of the Intergovernmental Panel on Climate Change*, edited by R. K Pachauri and A. Reisinger. Geneva, 2007.

———. "Summary for Policymakers." In *Climate Change 2007: The Physical Science Basis. Contribution of Working Group I to the Fourth Assessment Report of the Intergovernmental Panel on Climate Change*, edited by S. Solomon et al. Cambridge: Cambridge University Press, 2007.

Karl, Thomas, Susan J. Hassol, Christopher D. Miller, and William L. Murray, eds. *Temperature Trends in the Lower Atmosphere: Steps for*

Understanding and Reconciling Differences. A Report by the Climate Change Science Program and the Subcommittee on Global Change Research, Washington, DC, 2006.

Lüthi, Dieter, et al. "High-Resolution Carbon Dioxide Concentration Recorded 650,000-800,000 Years Before Present." *Nature* 453 (2008): 379–82.

Petit, J. R., et al. "Climate and Atmospheric History of the Past 420,000 Years from the Vostok Ice Core, Antarctica." *Nature* 399 (1999): 429–36.

Sherwood, Steven C., Cathryn L. Meyer, Robert J. Allen, and Holly A. Titchner. "Robust Tropospheric Warming Revealed by Iteratively Homogenized Radiosonde Data." *Journal of Climate* 21:20 (2008): 5336–52.

Tans, Pieter. "Trends in Atmospheric Carbon Dioxide—Mauna Loa." NOAA/ESRL. http://www.esrl.noaa.gov/gmd/ccgg/trends (accessed February 18, 2009).

CHAPTER 8. We've Done It Before

Andreae, Meinrat O. "Atmospheric Aerosols Versus Greenhouse Gases in the Twenty-First Century." *Philosophical Transactions of the Royal Society* 365:1856 (2007): 1915–23.

DOE/Argonne National Laboratory. "Improving Air Quality For 2008 Beijing Olympics." *ScienceDaily*, April 16, 2007. http://www.sciencedaily.com/releases/2007/04/070413102036.htm (accessed February 18, 2009).

Farman, J. C., B. G. Gardiner, and J. D. Shanklin. "Large Losses of Total Ozone in Antarctica Reveal Seasonal ClOx/NOx Interaction." *Nature* 315 (1985): 207–10.

Guillas, S., M. L. Stein, D. J. Wuebbles, and J. Xia. "Using Chemistry Transport Modeling in Statistical Analysis of Stratospheric Ozone Trends from Observations." *Journal of Geophysical Research* 109 (2004): D22303.

Mishchenko, Michael I. "Long-Term Satellite Record Reveals Likely Recent Aerosol Trend." *Science* 315:5818 (2007): 1543.

Ozone Hole. "Ozone Hole History." http://www.theozonehole.com/ozoneholehistory.htm (accessed February 18, 2009).

Reinsel, G. C., et al. "Trend Analysis of Total Ozone Data for Turnaround and Dynamical Contributions." *Journal of Geophysical Research Atmospheres* 110 (2005): D16306.

Stanhill, Gerald, and Shabtai Cohen. "Global Dimming: A Review of the Evidence for a Widespread Reduction in Global Radiation with Discussion of Its Probable Causes and Possible Agricultural Consequences." *Agricultural and Forest Meteorology* 107:4 (2001): 255–78.

Stolarski, R. S., et al. "Nimbus 7 Satellite Measurements of the Springtime Antarctic Ozone." *Nature* 322 (1986): 808–11.

Streets, D. G., Y. Wu, and M. Chin. "Two-Decadal Aerosol Trends as a Likely Explanation of the Global Dimming/Brightening Transition." *Geophysical Research Letters* 33 (2006): L15806.

United States Conference of Catholic Bishops. "Global Climate Change: A Plea for Dialogue, Prudence, and the Common Good." *A Statement of the United States Conference of Catholic Bishops,* June 15, 2001. http://www.usccb.org/sdwp/international/globalclimate.shtml.

Urbinato, David. "London's Historic 'Pea-Soupers.'" *EPA Journal* (2004). http://www.epa.gov/history/topics/perspect/london.htm (accessed February 18, 2009).

Wikipedia. "Thomas Midgley, Jr." http://en.wikipedia.org/wiki/Thomas_Midgley,_Jr. (accessed February 18, 2009).

Wild, M., A. Ohmura, and K. Makowski. "Impact of Global Dimming and Brightening on Global Warming." *Geophysical Research Letters* 34 (2007): L04702.

Wild, Martin. "From Dimming to Brightening: Decadal Changes in Solar Radiation at Earth's Surface." *Science* 308:5723 (2005): 847–50.

CHAPTER 9. *Weather Is Not Climate*

Climate Science: Roger Pielke Sr. Research Group News Blog. "TRMM (Tropical Rainfall Measuring Mission) Data Set Potential in Climate Controversy by Joanne Simpson, Private Citizen." http://climatesci .org/2008/02/27/trmm-tropical-rainfall-measuring-mission-data-set-potential-in-climate-controversy-by-joanne-simpson-private-citizen/.

Goddard Institute for Space Studies. "Global Temperature Trends: 2007 Summation." NASA Goddard Institute for Space Studies. August 12, 2008. data.giss.nasa.gov/gistemp/2007/.

Gunter, Lorne. "Forget Global Warming: Welcome to the New Ice Age." *National Post,* op ed, February 25, 2008. http://www.nationalpost .com/opinion/columnists/story.html?id=332289.

McCarthy, Leslie. "2007 Was Tied as Earth's Second Warmest Year." NASA Goddard Institute for Space Studies. January 16, 2008. http:// www.giss.nasa.gov/research/news/20080116/.

Met Office. "Climate Change and Global Variability." News release, March 5, 2008. http://www.metoffice.gov.uk/corporate/pressoffice/2008/ pr20080305.html.

———. "Cold Start to Winter." News release, December 12, 2008. http:// www.metoffice.gov.uk/corporate/pressoffice/2008/pr20081212.html.

———. "Is Global Warming All Over?" News release, April 29, 2008. http:// www.metoffice.gov.uk/corporate/pressoffice/2008/pr20081212.html.

National Climatic Data Center. "Climate of 2008 February in Historical Perspective Including Boreal Winter." March 13, 2008. http://www .ncdc.noaa.gov/oa/climate/research/2008/feb/global.html.

CHAPTER 10. The Natural Way of Things

Abdussamatov, H. I. "On Long-Term Variations of the Total Irradiance and on Probable Changes of Temperature in the Sun's Core." *Kinematika i Fizika Nebesnykh Tel* 21:6. (2005): 471–77.

Arctic Climate Impact Assessment. *Synthesis Report.* Cambridge: Cambridge University Press, 2005.

Arrhenius, Svante. "On the Influence of Carbonic Acid in the Air Upon the Temperature of the Ground." *Philosophical Magazine* 41 (1896): 237–76.

Caillon, Nicolas. "Timing of Atmospheric CO_2 and Antarctic Temperature Changes Across Termination III." *Science* 299:5613 (2003): 1728–31.

Callendar, G. S. "The Artificial Production of Carbon Dioxide and Its Influence on Climate." *Quarterly Journal of the Royal Meteorological Society* 64 (1938): 223–40.

———. "Can Carbon Dioxide Influence Climate?" *Weather* 4 (1949): 310–14.

———. "Infra-Red Absorption by Carbon Dioxide, with Special Reference to Atmospheric Radiation." *Quarterly Journal of the Royal Meteorological Society* 67 (1941): 263–75.

Commission on Presidential Debates. "The Biden-Palin Vice Presidential Debate." Debate transcript. http://www.debates.org/pages/trans2008b .html October 2, 2008.

Cook, John. "Are We Heading into a New Little Ice Age?" Skeptical Science Blog, October 25, 2007. http://www.skepticalscience.com/Are-we-heading-into-a-new-Little-Ice-Age.html (accessed February 18, 2009).

GISS Surface Temperature Analysis. "Global Temperature Trends: 2008 Annual Summation." NASA Goddard Institute for Space Studies. January 13, 2009. http://data.giss.nasa.gov/gistemp/2008/ (accessed February 18, 2009).

Lüthi, Dieter, et al. "High-Resolution Carbon Dioxide Concentration Record 650,000-800,000 Years Before Present." *Nature* 453 (2008): 379–82.

Marchitto, Thomas M., et al. "Marine Radiocarbon Evidence for the Mechanism of Deglacial Atmospheric CO_2 Rise." *Science* 316:5830 (2007): 1456–59.

Petit, J. R., et al. "Climate and Atmospheric History of the Past 420,000 Years from the Vostok Ice Core, Antarctica." *Nature* 399 (1999): 429–36.

Steig, Eric. "The Lag Between Temperature and CO_2. (Gore's Got It Right.)" Real Climate Blog, April 27, 2007. http://www.realclimate.org/index

.php/archives/2007/04/the-lag-between-temp-and-co2/ (accessed February 18, 2009).

Tyndall, John. "On Radiation Through the Earth's Atmosphere." *Philosophical Magazine* 4:25 (1863): 200–206.

——. "On the Absorption and Radiation of Heat by Gases and Vapours..." *Philosophical Magazine* 4:22 (1861): 169–94, 273–85.

Usoskin, I. G., S. K Solanki, and G. A. Kovaltsov. "Grand Minima and Maxima of Solar Activity: New Observational Constraints." *Astronomy and Astrophysics* 471:1 (2007): 301–9.

Weart, Spencer R. "The Carbon Dioxide Greenhouse Effect." In *The Discovery of Global Warming*. Cambridge, MA: Harvard University Press, 2003.

CHAPTER 11. No More Debate

American Association for the Advancement of Science. "AAAS Board Statement on Climate Change." December 9, 2006. http://www.aaas.org/news/press_room/climate_change/mtg_200702/aaas_climate_statement.pdf.

Ball, Jim. "Interview with Sir John Houghton on the Mall in Washington, DC." *Creation Care Magazine*, March 11, 2005.

Bolt, Andrew. ABC Television, "Bolt's Minority View," 2006. http://www.abc.net.au/mediawatch/transcripts/s1777013.htm.

Council of the American Quaternary Association (AMQUA). "Forum: Petroleum Geologists' Award to Novelist Crichton Is Inappropriate." *EOS* 87:36, September 5, 2006.

Cullen, H. M., P. B. deMenocal, S. Hemming, G. Hemming, F. H. Brown, T. Guilderson, and F. Sirocko. "Climate Change and the Collapse of the Akkadian Empire: Evidence from the Deep Sea." *Geology* 28:4 (2000): 379–82.

Doran, Peter T., and Maggie Kendall Zimmerman. "Examining the Scientific Consensus on Climate Change." *EOS* 90:3, January 20, 2009.

Global Research. "Scientists Abandon Global Warming 'Lie': 650 to Dissent at U.N. Climate Change Conference." December 13, 2008. http://www.globalresearch.ca/index.php?context=va&aid=11383.

Haug, Gerald H., Detlef Gunther, Larry C. Peterson, Daniel M. Sigman, Konrad A. Hughen, and Beat Aeschlimann. "Climate and the Collapse of Maya Civilization." *Science* 299:5613 (2003) 1731–35.

Lou Dobbs Tonight. CNN transcripts, January 13, 2009. http://transcripts.cnn.com/TRANSCRIPTS/0901/13/ldt.01.html.

Oregon Institute of Science and Medicine. "Global Warming Petition Project: Research Review of Global Warming Evidence." http://web

.archive.org/web/20070329084247/http://www.oism.org/oism/s32p31. htm/ http://www.oism.org/pproject/s33p37.htm.

Oreskes, Naomi. "Beyond the Ivory Tower: The Scientific Consensus on Climate Change." *Science* 306: 5702 (2004): 1686.

Petition Project. "Global Warming Petition Project." http://petitionproject.org/.

Robinson, Arthur B., Noah E. Robinson, and Willie Soon. "Environmental Effects of Increased Atmospheric Carbon Dioxide." *Journal of American Physicians and Surgeons* 12:3 (2007). http://www.jpands .org/vol12no3/robinson.pdf.

Scientific American, "Skepticism About Skeptics," August 23, 2006. http://web.archive.org/web/20060823125025/http://www.sciam .com/page.cfm?section=sidebar&articleID=0004F43C-DC1A-1C6E- 84A9809EC588EF21.

U.S. Climate Change Science Program. "Weather and Climate Extremes in a Changing Climate. Regions of Focus: North America, Hawaii, Caribbean, and U.S. Pacific Islands. Synopsis." http://downloads.climatescience .gov/sap/sap3-3/sap3-3-final-ExecutiveSummary.pdf.

Wikipedia. "Scientific opinion on climate change." http://en.wikipedia.org/ wiki/Scientific_opinion_on_climate_change#Academies_of_Science.

CHAPTER 12. *A Window to Our Climate Future*

Christensen, J. H., et al. "Regional Climate Projections." In *Climate Change 2007: The Physical Science Basis. Contribution of Working Group I to the Fourth Assessment Report of the Intergovernmental Panel on Climate Change*, edited by S. Solomon et al. Cambridge: Cambridge University Press, 2007.

Denman, K. L., et al. "Couplings Between Changes in the Climate System and Biogeochemistry." *Climate Change 2007: The Physical Science Basis. Contribution of Working Group I to the Fourth Assessment Report of the Intergovernmental Panel on Climate Change*, edited by S. Solomon et al. Cambridge: Cambridge University Press, 2007.

Hayhoe, K., D. Wuebbles, and C. Hayhoe. (Summary of Report). "Climate Change and Chicago: Projections and Potential Impacts. Research Summary Report." Chicago Climate Action, June 2008. http://www .chicagoclimateaction.org/filebin/pdf/report/Chicago_Climate_ Change_Impacts_Summary_June_2008.pdf.

Intergovernmental Panel on Climate Change (IPCC). "Special Report on Emissions Scenarios." 2001. http://www.grida.no/publications/other/ ipcc_sr/?src=/climate/ipcc/emission/.

Lyndersen, Kari. "Scientists: Pace of Climate Change Exceeds Estimates." *Washington Post*, February 15, 2009.

Parris, Brett. "World Vision Australia's Policy Position on Climate Change." World Vision. December 3, 2007.

Seager, R., et al. "Model Projections of an Imminent Transition to a More Arid Climate in Southwestern North America." *Science* 316:5828 (2007): 1181–84.

Van Vuuren, Detlef P., and Brian C. O'Neill. "The Consistency of IPCC's SRES Scenarios to 1990–2000 Trends and Recent Projections." *Climatic Change* 75 (2006): 1–2.

Walter, K. M., et al. "Methane Bubbling from Siberian Thaw Lakes as a Positive Feedback to Climate Warming." *Nature* 443 (2006): 71–75.

CHAPTER 13. *Increasing Extremes*

AFP. "Australian Wildfire Ferocity Linked to Climate Change: Experts." http://www.google.com/hostednews/afp/article/ALeqM5hCZR0o47pyQmTugqcds5ib6y-Esg (accessed March 5, 2009).

Andersen, Christine F., et al. "The New Orleans Hurricane Protection System: What Went Wrong and Why." PDF, 2007. American Society of Civil Engineers Hurricane Katrina External Review Panel. http://www.asce.org/files/pdf/ERPreport.pdf.

Bindoff, N. L., et al. "Observations: Oceanic Climate Change and Sea Level." In *Climate Change 2007: The Physical Science Basis. Contribution of Working Group I to the Fourth Assessment Report of the Intergovernmental Panel on Climate Change*, edited by S. Solomon. Cambridge: Cambridge University Press, 2007.

Bureau of Meteorology. "More Heat for Southern NSW but Relief in Sight." Australian Government Bureau of Meteorology. http://www.bom.gov.au/announcements/media_releases/nsw/20090205.shtml (accessed March 5, 2009).

Cane, Mark A., et al. "Twentieth-Century Sea Surface Temperature Trends." *Science* 275:5302 (1997): 957–60.

Earth Observatory. "Exceptional Australian Heat Wave." NASA. http://earthobservatory.nasa.gov/IOTD/view.php?id=36900 (accessed March 5, 2009).

Frich, P., et al. "Observed Coherent Changes in Climatic Extremems During the Second Half of the Twentieth Century." *Climate Research* 19:3 (2002): 193–212.

Hoyos, C. D., P. A. Agudelo, P. J. Webster, and J. A. Curry. "Deconvolution of the Factors Contributing to the Increase in Global Hurricane Intensity." *Science* 312:5770 (2006) 94–97.

IPCC. *Climate Change 2007: Impacts, Adaptation, and Vulnerability. Contribution of Working Group II to the Third Assessment Report of the Intergovernmental Panel on Climate Change*, edited by Martin Parry et al. Cambridge: Cambridge University Press, 2007.

Kalkstein, L. S., J. S. Greene, D. Mills, and A. Perrin. "The Development of Analog European Heat Waves for U.S. Cities to Analyze Impacts on Heat-Related Mortality." *Bulletin of the American Meteorological Society* 89 (2008): 75–86.

Karoly, David. "Brush Fires and Extreme Heat in South-East Australia." Real Climate: Climate Science from Climate Scientists. February 16, 2009. http://www.realclimate.org/index.php/archives/2009/02/bushfires -and-climate/.

Kiktev, Dmitry, David M. H. Sexton, Lisa Alexander, and Chris K. Folland. "Comparison of Modeled and Observed Trends in Indices of Daily Climate Extremes." *Journal of Climate* 16:22 (2003): 3560–71.

Knabb, Richard D, Jamie R. Rhome, and Daniel P. Brown. "Tropical Cyclone Report: Hurricane Katrina: 23–30 August 2005." PDF, December 20, 2005; updated August 10, 2006. National Hurricane Center. http://www.nhc.noaa.gov/pdf/TCR-AL122005_Katrina.pdf.

Lucas, C., K. Hennessy, G. Mills, and J. Bathols. "Bushfire Weather in Southeast Australia: Recent Trends and Projected Climate Change Impacts." In *Consultancy Report prepared for the Climate Institute of Australia by the Bushfire CRC and CSIRO*. Melbourne: Bushfire Cooperative Research Centre, 2007.

Mann, Michael E., and Kerry A. Emanuel. "Atlantic Hurricane Trends Linked to Climate Change." *EOS* 87:24 (2006). http://www.agu.org/pubs/crossref/2006/2006EO240001.shtml.

McLaren, Warren. "Australian Heatwave: 'Climate Change Link Is Very Likely.'" *Travel & Nature*, February 8, 2009.

National Climate Centre. "The Exceptional January–February 2009 Heatwave in Southeastern Australia." *Bureau of Meteorology, Special Climate Statement 17*. Melbourne: Bureau of Meteorology. 2009.

New Scientist. "Climate Models Predicted Australian Bushfires." February 15, 2009.

Nicholls, Neville, and Lisa Alexander. "Has the Climate Become More Variable or Extreme? Progress 1992–2006." *Progress in Physical Geography* 31:1 (2007): 77–87.

NOAA Satellite and Information Service. "Climate of 2005 Atlantic Hurricane Season." http://www.ncdc.noaa.gov/oa/climate/research/2005/hurricanes05.html.

Robine, Jean-Marie, et al. "Death Toll Exceeded 70,000 in Europe During the Summer of 2003 / Plus de 70 000 décès en Europe au cours de l'été 2003." *C. R. Biologies* 331 (2008).

Schwartz, John. "Army Admits Design Flaws in New Orleans Levee System: Corps of Engineers' Report Catalogs Years of Poor Planning and Construction Failures." *San Francisco Chronicle*, June 2, 2006.

Stott, Peter A., D. A. Stone, and M. R. Allen. "Human Contribution to the European Heatwave of 2003." *Nature* 432 (2004): 610–14.

Takver. "Climate Change Contributes to Catastrophic Australian Bushfires." *Sydney Indymedia*. February 8, 2009.

Tebaldi, Claudia, Katharine Hayhoe, Julie M. Arblaster, and Gerald A. Meehl. "Going to the Extremes: An Intercomparison of Model-Simulated Historical and Future Changes in Extreme Events." *Climatic Change* 79 (2006): 3–4.

Trenberth, K. E., et al. "Observations: Surface and Atmospheric Climate Change." In *Climate Change 2007: The Physical Science Basis. Contribution of Working Group I to the Fourth Assessment Report of the Intergovernmental Panel on Climate Change*, edited by S. Solomon et al. Cambridge: Cambridge University Press, 2007.

Trenberth, Kevin. "Uncertainty in Hurricanes and Global Warming." *Science* 308: 5729 (2005): 1753–54.

U.S. Army Corps of Engineers. "IPET: Risk and Reliability Report." http://nolarisk.usace.army.mil/.

Webster, P. J., G. J. Holland, J. A. Curry, and H. R. Chang. "Changes in Tropical Cyclone Number, Duration, and Intensity in a Warming Environment." *Science* 309: 5742 (2005): 1844–46.

CHAPTER 14. Water: Feast or Famine

ABARE. *Australian Crop and Livestock Report: October 2007 Drought Update*. Canberra: Australian Bureau of Agricultural and Resource Economics, 2007.

African Church Leaders' Statement On Climate Change and Water. www.kairoscanada.org/fileadmin/fe/files/PDF/EcoJustice/Climate/Statement_AfricanChurchLeaders-ClimateChange_June08.pdf (accessed March 5, 2009).

Alexander, L.V., et al. "Global observed changes in daily climate extremes of temperature and precipitation." *Journal of Geophysical Research-Atmospheres* 111 (2006).

Amos, Jonathan. "Creating the perfect firestorm." BBC News, February 10, 2009. http://news.bbc.co.uk/2/hi/asia-pacific/7879141.stm.

Barnett, T. P., J. C. Adam, and D. P. Lettenmaier. "Potential Impacts of a Warming Climate on Water Availability in Snow-Dominated Regions." *Nature* 438 (2005): 303–9.

BBC News, "Country profile: Tuvalu." http://news.bbc.co.uk/2/hi/asia-pacific/country_profiles/1249549.stm.

California Office of the Governor. "Executive Order S-3-05." http://gov.ca.gov/index.php?/executive-order/1861/.

Carrasco, J. F., G. Casassa, and J. Quintana. "Changes of the 0 Degree C Isotherm and the Equilibrium Lin Altitude in Central Chile During the Last quarter of the 20th Century." *Hydrological Sciences Journal* 50 (2005): 933–48.

Copeland, Larry. "Drought Spreading in Southeast." *USA Today*, February 12, 2008. http://www.usatoday.com/weather/drought/2008-02-11-drought_N.htm.

Goodman, Brenda. "Drought-Stricken South Facing Tough Choices." *New York Times*, October 16, 2007. http://www.nytimes.com/2007/10/16/us/16drought.html.

Gu, Guojun, et al. "Tropical Rainfall Variability on Interannual-to-Interdecadal and Longer Time Scales Derived from the GPCP Monthly Product." *Journal of Climate* 20 (2007): 4033–46.

Hayhoe, K., et al. "Emissions Pathways, Climate Change, and Impacts on California." *Proceedings of the National Academy of Sciences* 101 (2004): 12422–27.

Independent Online. "Wars Pale Against Natural Disasters—Expert." http://www.iol.co.za/index.php?set_id=1&click_id=143&art_id=nw20070828142036161C403888 (accessed March 5, 2009).

IPCC. *Climate Change Impacts and Adaptation.* New York: IPCC, 2007.

IPCC. *Climate Change 2007: The Physical Science Basis.* New York: IPCC, 2007.

Kaye, Nick. "While Supplies Last: Three Natural Wonders That Are Feeling the Heat." *New York Times*, June 26, 2005. http://travel.nytimes.com/2005/06/26/travel/26melt.html?_r=1&scp=1&sq=while%20supplies%20last&st=cse.

Kunkel, Kenneth E. "North American Trends in Extreme Precipitation." *Natural Hazards* 29 (2003): 291–305.

McGranahan, Gordon, Deborah Balk, and Bridget Anderson. "The Rising Tide: Assessing the Risks of Climate Change and Human Settlements in Low Elevation Coastal Zones." *Environment and Urbanization* 19 (2007): 17–37.

McGuire, Virginia L. "Water-Level Changes in the High Plains Aquifer, Predevelopment to 2005 and 2003 to 2005." *U.S. Geological Survey Scientific Investigations Report* 2006-5324: 2007.

Murphy, Bradley F., and Bertrand Timbal. "A Review of Recent Climate Variability and Climate Change in Southeastern Australia." *International Journal of Climatology* 28 (2008): 859–79.

Patel, Samir S. "News Feature: A Sinking Feeling." *Nature* 440 (2006): 734–36.

Reuters. "Peru Bets on Desalination to Ensure Water Supplies." March 11, 2008. http://www.reuters.com/article/environmentNews/idUSN11615837 20080312.

Schiermeier, Quirin. "Water: Purification with a Pinch of Salt." *Nature* 452 (2008): 260–61.

Seager, Richard, et al. "Model Projections of an Imminent Transition to a More Arid Climate in Southwestern North America." *Science* 316:5828 (2007): 1181–84.

Stewart, Iris T., Daniel R. Cayan, and Michael Dettinger. "Changes Towards Earlier Streamflow Timing Across Western North America." *Journal of Climate* 18 (2005): 1136–55.

Struck, Doug. "On the Roof of Peru, Omens in the Ice." *Washington Post*, July 29, 2006. http://www.washingtonpost.com/wp-dyn/content/article/2006/07/28/AR2006072801994_pf.html.

Vuille, Mathias, et al. "Climate Change and Tropical Andean Glaciers: Past, Present, and Future." *Earth-Science Reviews* 89 (2008): 79–96.

WGMS. "Global Glacier Changes: Facts and Figures." Zurich, Switzerland: World Glacier Monitoring Service, 2008.

Whittlesea. "Miracles and Misery for Bewildered Australians." *Financial Times*, February 14, 2009. http://www.ft.com/cms/s/0/c7769af6-fa38-11dd-9daa-000077b07658.html.

WWF. "An Overview of Glaciers, Glacier Retreat, and Subsequent Impacts in Nepal, India, and China." WWF Nepal Program: 2005.

CHAPTER 15. On Thin Ice

ACIA. "Arctic Climate Impact Assessment." Cambridge: Cambridge University Press: 2005.

Alley, Richard B. "Ice-Sheet and Sea-Level Changes." *Science* 310 (2005): 456–60.

BBC News. "Guide to Climate Change: Feedback Effects." http://news.bbc.co.uk/2/shared/spl/hi/sci_nat/04/climate_change/html/feedback.stm.

Bentley, Molly. "Earth's Permafrost Starts to Squelch." BBC News, December 29, 2004. http://news.bbc.co.uk/2/hi/science/nature/4120755.stm.

Chen, J. L., C. R. Wilson, and B. D. Tapley. "Satellite Gravity Measurements Confirm Accelerated Melting of Greenland Ice Sheet." *Science* 313 (2006): 1958–60.

Cook, A. J., A. J. Fox, D. G. Vaughan, and J. G. Ferrigno. "Retreating Glacier Fronts on the Antarctic Peninsula over the Past Half-Century." *Science* 308:5721 (2005): 541–44.

Derocher, Andrew E., Nicholas J. Lunn, and Ian Stirling. "Polar Bears in a Warming Climate." *Integrative and Comparative Biology* 44 (2004): 163–76.

Dowdeswell, Julian A. "The Greenland Ice Sheet and Global Sea-Level Rise." *Science* 311 (2006): 963–64.

essortment.com, "Polar Bear Watching." http://www.essortment.com/all/polarbearwatc_reql.htm.

Hesseldahl, Arik. "Who Owns Rights to a Melting Arctic?" *BusinessWeek*, January 28, 2009. http://www.businessweek.com/bwdaily/dnflash/content/jan2009/db20090127_954391.htm?chan=top+news_top+news+index+-+temp_news+%2B+analysis.

Holland, M. M., C. M. Bitz, and B. Tremblay. "Future Abrupt Reductions in the Summer Arctic Sea Ice." *Geophysical Research Letters* 33 (2006).

The Human Society of the United States. "Saving Acts for the Polar Bear." http://www.hsus.org/marine_mammals/a_closer_look_at_marine_mammals/polar_bears/saving_acts_for_the_polar.html.

International Agreement on the Conservation of Polar Bears. http://pbsg.npolar.no/ConvAgree/agreement.htm.

IPCC. *Climate Change 2007: The Physical Science Basis.* New York: IPCC, 2007.

The IUCN Red List of Threatened Species. "Ursus Maritimus." http://www.iucnredlist.org/details/22823.

Johannessen, Ola M., et al. "Ice-Sheet Growth in the Interior of Greenland." *Science* 310 (2005): 1013–16.

Lindsay, R. W., and J. Zhang. "The Thinning of Arctic Sea Ice, 1988–2003: Have We Passed a Tipping Point?" *Journal of Climate* 18 (2005): 4879–94.

Lindsay, R. W., et al. "Arctic Sea Ice Retreat in 2007 Follows Thinning Trend." *Journal of Climate* 22 (2009): 165–76.

Luckman, Adrian, et al. "Rapid and Synchronous Ice-Dynamic Changes in East Greenland." *Geophysical Research Letters* 33 (2006): L03503.

Min, Seung-Ki, Xuebin Zhang, and Francis Zwiers. "Human-Induced Arctic Moistening." *Science* 320 (2008): 518–20.

Monnett, Charles, and Jeffrey S. Gleason. "Observations of Mortality Associated with Extended Open-Water Swimming by Polar Bears in the Alaskan Beaufort Sea." *Polar Biology* 29 (2006): 681–87.

Motzfeldt, Josef. "Climate Change in a Greenlandic Perspective." Intuit Ataqatigiit. http://www.ia.gl/index.php?id=164&L=1 (accessed March 5, 2009).

Munro, Margaret. "Another Stunning Loss of Arctic Ice." Canada.com,

November 20, 2008. http://www.canada.com/technology/science/Another+stunning+loss+Arctic+report/976916/story.html.

National Snow and Ice Data Center. "Arctic Sea Ice News & Analysis." http://nsidc.org/arcticseaicenews/.

PBSG. *Proceedings of the 14th Working Meeting of the IUCN/SSC Polar Bear Specialist Group*, edited by J. Aars, N. J. Lunn, and A. E. Derocher. Seattle, WA: IUCN, 2006.

Preston, Diana. "Churchill, Canada: Polar Bear Capital." *Telegraph .co.uk*, August 26, 2008. http://www.telegraph.co.uk/travel/activityand adventure/2597713/Churchill-Canada-Polar-bear-capital.html.

Regehr, Eric V., et al. "Effects of Earlier Sea Ice Breakup on Survival and Population Size of Polar Bears in Western Hudson Bay." *Journal of Wildlife Management* 71 (2007): 2673–83.

Rignot, Eric, and Pannir Kanagaratnam. "Changes in the Velocity Structure of the Greenland Ice Sheet." *Science* 311 (2006): 986–90.

ScienceDaily. "Glaciers Around the Globe Continue to Melt at High Rates." February 4, 2009. http://www.sciencedaily.com/releases/2009/01/0901 29090002.htm.

Seguin, Rheal. "Scientists Predict Seasonal Ice-Free Arctic by 2015." *Globe and Mail*, December 12, 2008.

Truffer, Martin, and Mark Fahnestock. "Rethinking Ice Sheet Time Scales." *Science* 315 (2007): 1508–10.

Velicogna, Isabella, and John Wahr. "Measurements of Time-Variable Gravity Show Mass Loss in Antarctica." *Science* 311 (2006): 1754–56.

Wentz, Frank J., et al. "How Much More Rain Will Global Warming Bring?" *Science* 317 (2007): 233–35.

WWF. *Arctic Climate Impact Science: An Update Since ACIA*. Oslo, Norway, WWF International Arctic Programme: 2008.

CHAPTER 16. Rising Seas

BBC News. "Country profile: Tuvalu." http://news.bbc.co.uk/2/hi/asia -pacific/country_profiles/1249549.stm.

Beckley, B., et al. "A Reassessment of Global and Regional Mean Sea Level Trends from TOPEX and Jason-1 Altimetry Based on Revised Reference Frames and Orbits." *Geophysical Research Letters* 34:14 (2007): L14608.

Cabanes, C., A. Cazenave, and C. Le Provost. "Sea Level Rise During Past 40 Years Determined from Satellite and in Situ Observations." *Science* 294:5543 (2001): 840–42.

Dasgupta, Sasmita, et al. "World Bank: The Impact of Sea Level Rise on Developing Countries: A Comparative Analysis." http://econ.worldbank.org/

external/default/main?ImgPagePK=64202988&entityID=000016406_20
070209161430&pagePK=64165259&theSitePK=469382&piPK=585673.

IPCC. *Climate Change 2007: Impacts and Adaptation.* New York: IPCC, 2007.

———. *Climate Change 2007: The Physical Science Basis.* New York: IPCC, 2007.

McGranahan, Gordon, Deborah Balk, and Bridget Anderson. "The Rising Tide: Assessing the Risks of Climate Change and Human Settlements in Low Elevation Coastal Zones." *Environment and Urbanization* 19 (2007): 17–37.

Parris, Brett. "World Vision Australia's Policy Position on Climate Change." World Vision. December 3, 2007.

Patel, Samir S. "News Feature: A Sinking Feeling." *Nature* 440 (2006): 734–36.

Shepard, Andrew, and Duncan Wingham. "Recent Sea-Level Contributions of the Antarctic and Greenland Ice Sheets." *Science* 315 (2007): 1529–32.

Steig, Eric J., et al. "Warming of the Antarctic Ice-Sheet Surface Since the 1957 International Geophysical Year." *Nature* 457 (2009): 459–62.

Woodard, Colin. "Dutch Defy Seas, but Indulge Rivers." *Christian Science Monitor,* August 23, 2001. http://www.csmonitor.com/2001/0823/p17s1-sten.html.

World Vision. "Natural Disasters: World Vision Responds to Regional Crises Across the Globe." http://www.worldvision.org/news.nsf/news/200709_natural_disasters?Open&wvsrc=enews&lpos=main&lid=natural_disasters200709 (accessed March 5, 2009).

Worldwatch Institute. *Vital Signs 2003: The Trends That are Shaping Our Future.* New York: W. W. Norton, 2003.

CHAPTER 17. Our Fragile Food Chain

Amthor, Jeffrey S. "Effects of Atmospheric CO_2 Concentration on Wheat Yield: A Review of Results from Experiments Using Various Approaches to Control CO_2 Concentration." *Field Crops Research* 73 (2001): 1–34.

Asseng, S., et al. "Simulated Wheat Growth Affected by Rising Temperature, Increased Water Deficit and Elevated Atmospheric CO_2." *Field Crops Research* 85 (2004): 85–102.

Associated Press. "Climate Change Could Lead to Global Food Crisis, Scientists Warn." *International Herald Tribune,* April 10, 2008. http://www.iht.com/articles/ap/2008/04/10/europe/EU-GEN-Hungary-Climate-Change.php.

Beckley, B. D., et al. "A Reassessment of Global and Regional Mean Sea Level Trends from TOPEX and Jason-1 Altimetry Based on Revised Reference Frame and Orbits." *Geophysical Research Letters* 34:14 (2007): L14608.

Cabanes, C., A. Cazenave, and C. Le Provost. "Sea Level Rise During Past 40 Years Determined from Satellite and in Situ Observations." *Science* 294:5543 (2001): 840–42.

Case, Christa Farrand. "Climate Change Could Sour US Maple Sugaring." *Christian Science Monitor*, April 6, 2005. http://www.csmonitor.com/2005/0406/p11s01-sten.html.

Daley, Beth. "As Frost Fades, Berry Rivalry Heats: Temperatures Pit Maine, Quebec Growers." *Boston Globe*, October 1, 2007. http://www.boston.com/news/local/maine/articles/2007/10/01/as_frost_fades_berry_rivalry_heats/.

Dasgupta, Susmita, et al. "World Bank: The Impact of Sea Level Rise on Developing Countries: A Comparative Analysis." Research at the World Bank. http://econ.worldbank.org/external/default/main?ImgPagePK=64202988&entityID=000016406_20070209161430&pagePK=64165259&theSitePK=469382&piPK=585673 (accessed March 5, 2009).

Doyle, Alister. "Christians See Climate Change as Moral Issue." *Reuters*, August 23, 2008.

Easterling, W. E., et al. "Food, Fibre and Forest Products." In *Climate Change 2007: Impacts, Adaptation and Vulnerability. Contribution of Working Group II to the Fourth Assessment Report of the Intergovernmental Panel on Climate Change*, edited by M. L. Parry, et al., 273–313. Cambridge: Cambridge University Press, 2007.

Fischer, G., M. Shah, F. N. Tubiello, and H. van Velhuizen. "Socio-Economic and Climate Change Impacts on Agriculture: An Integrated Assessment, 1990–2080." *Philosophical Transactions of the Royal Society B* 360 (2005): 2067–83.

International Herald Tribune. "Global Food Crisis Called 'A Wake-Up Call' at UN Summit." *International Herald Tribune*, June 4, 2008. http://www.iht.com/articles/2008/06/04/news/food.php.

IPCC. *Climate Change 2007: The Physical Science Basis*. New York: IPCC, 2007.

Lobell, David B., and Christopher B. Field. "Global Scale Climate-Crop Yield Relationships and the Impacts of Recent Warming." *Environmental Research Letters* 2 (2007): 014002.

Long, Stephen P., et al. "Food for Thought: Lower-Than-Expected Crop Yield Stimulation with Rising CO_2 Concentrations." *Science* 312 (2006): 1918–21.

Lough, Richard. "Climate Change." World Vision Report. http://www

.worldvision.org/worldvision/radio.nsf/0/1A874F0FFCAF83DB
882573A80075EF30?OpenDocument (accessed March 5, 2009).

Metro East Coast Assessment Group. "US National Assessment of the Potential Consequences of Climate Variability and Change Region: Metro East Coast." Washington DC: US Climate Change Science Program / US Global Change Research Program, 2003.

Miller, Jack, and Fred Pearce. "Soviet Climatologist Predicts Greenhouse 'Paradise.' " *New Scientist*, August 29, 1989. http://www.newscientist.com/article/mg12316791.200-soviet-climatologist-predicts-greenhouse-paradise-.html.

Miller, Kenneth G. "The Phanerozoic Record of Global Sea-Level Change." *Science* 310:5752 (2005): 1293–98.

Mohan, Jacqueline E., et al. "Biomass and Toxicity Responses of Poison Ivy (Toxicodendron Radicans) to Elevated Atmospheric CO_2." *Proceedings of the National Academy of Sciences* 103 (2006): 9086–89.

Peng, Shaobing, et al. "Rice Yields Decline with Higher Night Temperature from Global Warming." *Proceedings of the National Academy of Sciences* 101 (2004): 9971–75.

Ramankutty, Navin, Jonathan A. Foley, John Norman, and Kevin McSweeney. "The Global Distribution of Cultivable Lands: Current Patterns and Sensitivity to Possible Climate Change." *Global Ecology and Biogeography* 11 (2002): 377–92.

Reilly, John, et al. "Global Economic Effects of Changes in Crops, Pasture, and Forests Due to Changing Climate, Carbon Dioxide and Ozone." *Energy Policy* 35 (2007): 5370–83.

Reuters. "Food Crisis, Silent Famine to Continue: World Bank." *Economic Times*, September 3, 2008. http://www.iht.com/articles/ap/2008/04/10/europe/EU-GEN-Hungary-Climate-Change.php.

Schimel, David. "Climate Change and Crop Yields: Beyond Cassandra." *Science* 312 (2006): 1889–90.

Tebaldi, C., and D. B. Lobell. "Towards Probabilistic Projections of Climate Change Impacts on Global Crop Yields." *Geophysical Research Letters* 35 (2008): L08705.

Vidal, John. "Global Food Crisis Looms as Climate Change and Fuel Shortages Bite." *Guardian*, November 3, 2007. http://www.guardian.co.uk/environment/2007/nov/03/food.climatechange.

Ziska, L. H. "Evaluation of Yield Loss in Field Sorghum from a C3 and C4 Weed with Increasing CO_2." *Weed Science* 51 (2003): 914–18.

———. "The Impact of Elevated CO_2 on Yield Loss from a C3 and C4 Weed in Field-Grown Soybean." *Global Change Biology* 6 (2000): 899–905.

Ziska, Lewis H., and Frances A. Caulfield. "Rising CO_2 and Pollen Production of Common Ragweed (Ambrosia Artemisiifolia L.), A Known Allergy-Inducing Species: Implications for Public Health." *Australian Journal of Plant Physiology* 27 (2000): 893–98.

CHAPTER 18. Squirrels and Seeds

African Church Leaders' Statement On Climate Change and Water. http://www.kairoscanada.org/fileadmin/fe/files/PDF/EcoJustice/ Climate/Statement_AfricanChurchLeaders-ClimateChange_June08 .pdf (accessed March 5, 2009).

Arbor Day Foundation. "Hardiness Zone Changes Between 1990 and 2004." http://www.arborday.org/media/map_change.cfm (accessed February 17, 2009).

———. "Hardiness Zones." http://www.arborday.org/media/zones.cfm (accessed February 17, 2009).

Beever, E. A, et al. "American Pikas (Ochotona Princeps) in Northwestern Nevada: A Newly Discovered Population at a Low-Elevation Site." *Western North American Naturalist* 68 no. 1 (2008): 8–14.

Beever, E. A., P. F. Brussard, and J. Berger. "Patterns of Extirpation Among Isolated Populations of Pikas (Ochotona Princeps) in the Great Basin." *Journal of Mammalogy* 84 (2003): 37–54.

Blaustein, R. J. "Kudzu's Invasion into Southern United States Life and Culture." In *The Great Reshuffling: Human Dimensions of Invasive Species*, edited by J. A. McNeeley, 55–62. Cambridge, MA: World Conservation Union, 2001.

Britton, Kerry, David Orr, and Jianghua Sun. "Kudzu." In *Invasive Plants of the Eastern United States*. http://www.invasive.org/eastern/ biocontrol/25Kudzu.html.

Cheung, W., et al. "The Capacity and Likelihood of Climate Change Adaptation in the World's Fisheries." *Fish and Fisheries*, 2008.

Confalonieri, U., et al. "Human Health." In *Climate Change 2007: Impacts, Adaptation and Vulnerability. Contribution of Working Group II to the Fourth Assessment Report of the Intergovernmental Panel on Climate Change*, edited by M. L. Parry, et al., 391–431. Cambridge: Cambridge University Press, 2007.

Fischlin, A., et al. "Ecosystems, Their Properties, Goods and Services." In *Climate Change 2007: Impacts, Adaptation and Vulnerability. Contribution of Working Group II to the Fourth Assessment Report of the Intergovernmental Panel on Climate Change*, edited by M.L. Parry et al., 211–72. Cambridge: Cambridge University Press, 2007.

Fitter, A. H., and R. Fitter. "Rapid Changes in Flowering Time in British plants." *Science* 296 (2002): 1689–91.

Forseth, I., and A.F. Innis. "Kudzu (Pueraria montana): History, Physiology, and Ecology Combine to Make a Major Ecosystem Threat." *Critical Reviews in Plant Sciences* 23 (2004): 401–13.

Francl, K., K. Hayhoe, M. Saunders, and E. Maurer. "Ecosystem Adaptation to Climate Change: Mammal Migration Pathways in the Great Lakes States." *Journal of Great Lakes Research* (2009: forthcoming).

Government of Saskatchewan. "The Mountain Pine Beetle—A Growing Concern." February 14, 2008. http://www.environment.gov.sk.ca/Default.aspx?DN=345f140a-746a-4fa3-9f49-e34ea60b31ba.

Hellmann, J., et al. "Climate Change Impacts on Terrestrial Ecosystems in Multi-State Region Centered on Chicago." *Journal of Great Lakes Research* (2009: forthcoming).

Huntington, T. "Climate Change, Growing Season Length, and Transpiration: Plant Response Could Alter Hydrologic Regime." *Plant Biology* 5 (2004): 651–53.

Iverson, L., A. Prasad, and S. Matthews. "Potential Changes in Suitable Habitat for 134 Species in the Northeastern United States." *Mitigation and Adaptation Strategies for Global Change* 13:5-6 (2008): 487–516.

Jay, Paul. "The Beetle and the Damage Done," *CBC News*, April 23, 2008. http://www.cbc.ca/news/background/science/beetle.html.

Kurz, W. A., et al. "Beetle Tree Kill Releases More Carbon than Fires." *Nature* 452 (2008): 987–90.

Linderholm, H. "Growing Season Changes in the Last Century." *Agricultural and Forest Meteorology* 137 (2006): 1–14.

Loarie S.R., et al. "Climate Change and the Future of California's Endemic Flora." *PLoS ONE* 3:6 (2008): e2502.

Miller-Rushing, A. J., et al. "Photographs and Herbarium Specimens as Tools to Document Phenological Changes in Response to Global Warming." *American Journal of Botany* 93 (2006): 1667–74.

Perry, Alison, Paula J. Low, Jim R. Ellis, and John D. Reynolds. "Climate Change and Distribution Shifts in Marine Fishes," *Science* 308:5730 (2005): 1912.

Pounds, J.A., et al. "Widespread Amphibian Extinctions from Epidemic Disease Driven by Global Warming." *Nature* 439 (2006): 161–67.

Primack, D., et al. "Herbarium Specimens Demonstrate Earlier Flowering Times in Response to Warming in Boston." *American Journal of Botany* 91 (2004): 1260–64.

Restoring Eden. "Our Mission." http://www.restoringeden/about (accessed March 5, 2009).

Root, T. L., et al. "Fingerprints of Global Warming on Wild Animals and Plants." *Nature* 421 (2003): 57–60.

Rosenzweig, C., et al. "Attributing Physical and Biological Impacts to Anthropogenic Climate Change." *Nature* 453 (2008): 353–57.

Taylor, S. W., A. L. Carroll, R. I. Alfaro, and L. Safranyik. "Forest, Climate and Mountain Pine Beetle Outbreak Dynamics in Western Canada." In *The Mountain Pine Beetle: A Synthesis of Biology, Management and Impacts in Lodgepole Pine*, edited by L. Safranyik and W. Wilson, 67–94. Natural Resources Canada, Canadian Forest Service, Pacific Forestry Centre, British Columbia, 2006.

Thomas, C.D., et al. "Extinction Risk from Climate Change." *Nature* 427 (2004): 145–48.

Weflen, Kathleen, 2001. "The Crossroads of Climate Change." Minnesota Department of Natural Resources. http://www.dnr.state.mn.us/volunteer/janfeb01/warming.html.

Wookey, P. "The Earth System: Biological and Ecological Dimensions of Global Environmental Change." In *Encyclopedia of Global Environmental Change*, vol. 2, edited by T. Munn. Chichester, UK: John Wiley & Sons, 2002.

CHAPTER 19. *Motivation for Change*

African Church Leaders' Statement On Climate Change and Water. http://www.kairoscanada.org/fileadmin/fe/files/PDF/EcoJustice/Climate/Statement_AfricanChurchLeaders-ClimateChange_June08.pdf (accessed March 5, 2009).

Arnell, Nigel W. "Climate Change and Global Water Resources: SRES Emissions and Socio-Economic Scenarios." *Global Environmental Change* 14:1 (2004): 31–52.

Biro, Peter A., John R. Post, and David J. Booth. "Mechanisms for Climate-Induced Mortality of Fish Populations in Whole-Lake Experiments." *Proceedings of the National Academy of Science* 104:23 (2006): 9715–19.

Brown, Molly E., and Christopher C. Funk. "Food Security Under Climate Change." *Science* 319 (2008): 580–81.

Carr, John L. "Religious and Moral Dimensions of Global Climate Change." Written Senate Testimony. June 7, 2007. epw.senate.gov/public/index.cfm?FuseAction=Files.View&FileStore_id=28110b16-da22-4304-8827-77e563de95f5 (accessed March 5, 2009).

Conisbee, Molly, and Andrew Simms. *Environmental Refugees: The Case for Recognition*. London: New Economics Foundation, 2003.

De Wit, Maarten, et al. "Changes in Surface Water Supply Across Africa with Predicted Climate Change." *Science* 311 (2006): 1917.

Easterling, W. E., et al. "Food, Fibre and Forest Products." In *Climate Change 2007: Impacts, Adaptation and Vulnerability. Contribution of Working Group II to the Fourth Assessment Report of the Intergovernmental Panel on Climate Change*, edited by M. L. Parry, et al., 273–313. Cambridge: Cambridge University Press, 2007.

Hoerner, J. Andrew, and Nia Robinson. *A Climate of Change African Americans, Global Warming, and a Just Climate Policy for the U.S.* Oakland, CA: Environmental Justice and Climate Change Initiative, 2008.

Kundzewicz, Z. W., et al. "Freshwater Resources and Their Management." In *Climate Change 2007: Impacts, Adaptation and Vulnerability. Contribution of Working Group II to the Fourth Assessment Report of the Intergovernmental Panel on Climate Change*, edited by M. L. Parry, 173–210. Cambridge: Cambridge University Press, 2007.

Parry, M. L., et al. "Effects of Climate Change on Global Food Production Under SRES Emissions and Socio-Economic Scenarios." *Global Environmental Change* 14:1 (2004): 53–67.

Patz, Jonathan A., Diarmid Campbell-Lendrum, Tracey Holloway, and Jonathan A. Foley. "Impact of Regional Climate Change on Human Health." *Nature* 438:17 (2005): 310–17.

World Health Organization. "The World Health Report 2002—Reducing Risks, Promoting Healthy Life." http://www.who.int/whr/2002/en/.

CHAPTER 20. *No Fear in Life*

Farley, Andrew Prather. *The Naked Gospel*. Grand Rapids: Zondervan, forthcoming.

CHAPTER 21. *Spiritual Freedom, Wisdom, and Compassion*

Southern Baptist Environment & Climate Initiative. "A Southern Baptist Declaration on the Environment and Climate Change." http://www.baptistcreationcare.org/node/1 (accessed March 5, 2009).

CHAPTER. 22. *Small Steps Toward Change*

Consumer Reports. "Greener Choices: Products for a Better Planet." http://www.greenerchoices.org/.

Energy Star. "Compact Fluorescent Light Bulbs for Consumers." http://www.energystar.gov/index.cfm?c=cfls.pr_cfls.

Gardner, Gerald T., and Paul C. Stern. "The Short List: The Most Effective Actions U.S. Households Can Take to Curb Climate Change." *Environment*, September/October 2008.

Hybrid Cars. "All Hybrid Car Models and Efficient Vehicles." October 2008. http://www.hybridcars.com/hybrid-cars-list.

International Herald Tribune. "UN Says Half the World's Population Will Live in Urban Areas by End of 2008." February 26, 2008. http://www.iht .com/articles/ap/2008/02/26/news/UN-GEN-UN-Growing-Cities.php.

National Public Radio. "Climate Change: An Evangelical Call to Action." February 2006. http://www.npr.org/documents/2006/feb/evangelical/ calltoaction.pdf (accessed March 5, 2009).

United Nations. "World Urbanization Prospects: The 2007 Revision Population Database." http://esa.un.org/unup/index.asp?panel=1.

United States Environmental Protection Agency (EPA). "Purchasing An Energy Star Computer." July 1994. http://www.fs.fed.us/sustainable-operations/documents/EPA-PurchasingAnEnergyStarComputer.pdf.

———. "Sleep, Does a Body and the Environment Good Energy Star Launches Low Carbon IT Campaign." April 2008. http://yosemite .epa.gov/opa/admpress.nsf/dc57b08b5acd42bc852573c90044a9c4/ 0bda6ac3a293fb6e85257420004aa066!OpenDocument.

The University of New South Wales. "Standby Power—You're Paying for It!" http://www.energy.unsw.edu.au/NewsInfoStandbyPower.shtml.

U.S. Department of Energy: Energy Efficiency and Renewable Energy. "Energy Savers: Home Office and Home Electronics." http://www1 .eere.energy.gov/consumer/tips/home_office.html.

———. "Water Heating." http://www.energy.gov/waterheating.htm.

U.S. Department of Transportation: Federal Highway Administration. "Census 2000 Population Statistics." http://www.fhwa.dot.gov/planning/ census/cps2k.htm.

Walsh, Bryan. "Building Green Houses for the Poor." *Time*, Feb. 17, 2009, Health and Science section.

World Development Movement. "Desmond Tutu on Climate Change." http:// www.youtube.com/watch?v=onSHD4sAuB4 (accessed March 5, 2009).

CHAPTER 23. *Taking On the World*

Batson, Andrew. "Chinese Entrepreneur Makes Good at Home," *Pittsburgh Post-Gazette*, October 12, 2006. http://www.post-gazette.com/ pg/06285/729737-82.stm.

CBC News. "Don't Call Them the Big Three; They're the Detroit Three—For Now," February 17, 2009. http://www.cbc.ca/money/story/2009/ 02/17/f-bigthreeupdate.html.

Friedman, Thomas L. *Hot, Flat, and Crowded: Why We Need a Green Revolution—and How It Can Renew America.* New York: Farrar, Straus & Giroux, 2008.

Graham, Billy. *Approaching Hoofbeats*. New York: Avon, 1985.

IPCC. "Summary for Policymakers." In *Climate Change 2007: Impacts, Adaptation and Vulnerability. Contribution of Working Group II to the Fourth Assessment Report of the Intergovernmental Panel on Climate Change*, edited by M. L. Parry et al., 7–22. Cambridge: Cambridge University Press, 2007.

———. "Summary for Policymakers." In *Climate Change 2007: Mitigation. Contribution of Working Group III to the Fourth Assessment Report of the Intergovernmental Panel on Climate Change*, edited by B. Metz. Cambridge: Cambridge University Press. 2007.

John Paul II, Pope. "Post-Synodal Apostolic Exhortation, Ecclesia in Asia, of the Holy Father John Paul II to the Bishops, Priests and Deacons, Men and Women in the Consecrated Life and All the Lay Faithful on Jesus Christ the Savior and His Mission of Love and Service in Asia: 'That They May Have Life, and Have It Abundantly' (Jn 10:10)." Environmental Quotes. http://conservation.catholic.org/more_pope_john_paul_ii.htm (accessed March 5, 2009).

Kling, George W., et al, 2003. A Report of the Union of Concerned Scientists. "Confronting Climate Change in the Great Lakes Region: Impacts on Our Communities and Ecosystems." http://www.ucsusa.org/greatlakes/.

Langford, Ian H., and Graham Bentham. "The Potential Effects of Climate Change on Winter Mortality in England and Wales." *Biometeorology* 28:3 (1995): 141–47.

MSNBC. "Carmakers Lose Lawsuit on Carbon Emission," September 12, 2007: http://www.msnbc.msn.com/id/20746463/.

Pacala, S., and R. Socolaw. "Stabilization Wedges: Solving the Climate Problem for the Next 50 Years with Current Technologies." *Science* 205 (2004): 968–72.

Wall Street Journal. "Sales and Share of Total Market by Manufacturer." February 3, 2009. http://online.wsj.com/mdc/public/page/2_3022-autosales.html#autosalesE.

Watts, Jonathan. "Bright Future for China's Solar Billionaire," *Guardian*, July 25, 2008. http://www.guardian.co.uk/global/2008/jul/25/solarpower.alternativeenergy.

FIGURES

Alley, R. B. "GISP2 Ice Core Temperature and Accumulation Data." NOAA/NGDC Paleoclimatology Program, Boulder CO, USA. (2004) Available online at: http://ftp.ncdc.noaa.gov/pub/data/paleo/icecore/greenland/summit/gisp2/isotopes/gisp2_temp_accum_alley2000.txt.

————. "The Younger Dryas Cold Interval as Viewed from Central Greenland." *Quaternary Science Reviews* 19 (2000): 213–26.

Becker, J. J., et al. "Global Bathymetry and Elevation Data at 30 Arc Seconds Resolution: SRTM30_PLUS." *Marine Geodesy* (2009: forthcoming).

Brohan, P., et al. "Uncertainty Estimates in Regional and Global Observed Temperature Changes: A New Dataset from 1850." *Journal of Geophysical Research* 111 (2006): D12106.

Church, J. A., and N. J. White. "A 20th Century Acceleration in Global Sea-Level Rise." *Geophysical Research Letters* 33 (2006): L01602.

Climate Analysis Indicators Tool (CAIT) version 3.0. Washington, DC: World Resources Institute, 2005. Available at http://cait.wri.org.

Dai, A., K. E. Trenberth, and T. Qian. "A Global Data Set of Palmer Drought Severity Index for 1870–2002: Relationship with Soil Moisture and Effects of Surface Warming." *Journal of Hydrometeorology* 5 (2004): 1117–30.

EIA. *International Energy Annual 2005.* Available online at http://www.eia.doe.gov/iea/carbon.html.

Emanuel, K. "Increasing Destructiveness of Tropical Cyclones Over the Past 30 Years." *Nature* 436 (2005): 686–88.

Fröhlich, C. "Observations of Irradiance Variations." *Space Science Reviews* 94 (2000): 15–24.

————. "Solar Irradiance Variability Since 1978: Revision of the PMOD Composite during Solar Cycle 21." *Space Science Reviews* 125:1-4 (2006): 53–65.

Hansen, J., et al. "Global Temperature Change." *Proceedings of the National Academy of Science* 103 (2006): 14288–93.

IAGA Bulletin. N° 32 I Geomagnetic Data 1981 in IAGA Indices: aa, Am, Kp, Dst, AE Rapid Variations IUGG Publications Office. 1988. Available online at ftp://ftp.ngdc.noaa.gov/STP/SOLAR_DATA/RELATED_INDICES/AA_INDEX/.

IEA. "CO_2 Emissions from Fuel Combustion." 2004. Available online at http://data.iea.org/ieastore/co2_main.asp.

IPCC. "Summary for Policymakers." In *Climate Change 2007: The Physical Science Basis. Contribution of Working Group I to the Fourth Assessment Report of the Intergovernmental Panel on Climate Change,* edited by S. Solomon et. al. Cambridge: Cambridge University Press, 2007.

Jouzel, J., et al. "A New 27 Ky High Resolution East Antarctic Climate Record." *Geophysical Research Letters* 28:16 (2001): 3199–3202.

Keeling, C. D., et al. "Atmospheric Carbon Dioxide Variations at Mauna Loa Observatory, Hawaii." *Tellus* 28:6 (1976): 538–51.

Keeling, R. F., S. C. Piper, A. F. Bollenbacher, and J. S. Walker. "Atmospheric CO_2 Records from Sites in the SIO Air Sampling Network."

In *Trends: A Compendium of Data on Global Change*. Carbon Dioxide Information Analysis Center, Oak Ridge National Laboratory, U.S. Department of Energy, Oak Ridge, Tenn., USA. 2008. Available online at http://cdiac.ornl.gov/trends/co2/sio-mlo.html.

Lea, D. W., D. K. Pak, L. C. Peterson, and K. A. Hughen. "Synchroneity of Tropical and High-Latitude Atlantic Temperatures over the Last Glacial Termination." *Science* 301:5638 (2003): 1361–64.

Lea, D. W., et al. "Cariaco Basin Foraminiferal Mg/Ca and SST Reconstruction." NOAA/NGDC Paleoclimatology Program, Boulder, CO, USA. 2003. Available online at ftp://ftp.ncdc.noaa.gov/pub/data/paleo/ contributions_by_author/lea2003/cariaco_2003.txt.

Mann, M. E., and P. D. Jones. "Global Surface Temperatures over the Past Two Millennia." *Geophysical Research Letters* 30:15 (2003): L1820.

———. "2,000 Year Hemispheric Multi-proxy Temperature Reconstructions." NOAA/NGDC Paleoclimatology Program, Boulder CO, USA. 2003. Available online at ftp://ftp.ncdc.noaa.gov/pub/data/paleo/ contributions_by_author/mann2003b/mann2003b.txt.

Marland, G., B. Andres, and T. Boden. *Global CO_2 Emissions from Fossil-Fuel Burning, Cement Manufacture, and Gas Flaring: 1751-2005*. Carbon Dioxide Information Analysis Center, Oak Ridge National Laboratory, Oak Ridge, Tennessee. 2008. Available online at http://cdiac.ornl.gov/trends/emis/overview.html.

Marland, G., T. A. Boden, and R. J. Andres. "Global, Regional, and National Fossil Fuel CO_2 Emissions." In *Trends: A Compendium of Data on Global Change*. Carbon Dioxide Information Analysis Center, Oak Ridge National Laboratory, U.S. Department of Energy, Oak Ridge, Tenn., USA. 2005. Available online at http://cdiac.esd.ornl.gov/ trends/emis/meth_reg.html.

McMichael, J., et al. "Global Climate Change." In *Comparative Quantification of Health Risks: Global and Regional Burden of Disease due to Selected Major Risk Factors*, edited by M. Ezzati, A. Lopez, A. Rodgers, and C. Murray. Geneva: World Health Organization, 2004.

Meehl, G. A., et al. "The WCRP CMIP3 Multi-Model Dataset: A New Era in Climate Change Research." *Bulletin of the American Meteorological Society* 88 (2007): 1383–94.

Neftel, A., et al. "Historical CO_2 Record from the Siple Station Ice Core." In *Trends: A Compendium of Data on Global Change*. Carbon Dioxide Information Analysis Center, Oak Ridge National Laboratory, U.S. Department of Energy, Oak Ridge, Tenn., USA. 1994. Available online at http://cdiac.ornl.gov/trends/co2/siple.html.

Neftel, A., E. Moor, H. Oeschger, and B. Stauffer. "Evidence from Polar Ice Cores for the Increase in Atmospheric CO_2 in the Past Two Centuries." *Nature* 315 (1985): 45–47.

Olivier, J. G., et al. "Recent Trends in Global Greenhouse Gas Emissions: Regional Trends and Spatial Distribution of Key Sources." In *Non-CO_2 Greenhouse Gases (NCGG-4)*, 325–30. Rotterdam: Millpress, 2005.

Pacala, S. and R. Socolow. "Stabilization Wedges: Solving the Climate Problem for the Next 50 Years with Current Technologies." *Science* 305:5686 (2004): 968–72.

Parker, D. E., T. P. Legg, and C. K. Folland. "A New Daily Central England Temperature Series, 1772–1991." *International Journal of Climatology* 12 (1992): 317–42.

Petit J. R., et al. "Climate and Atmospheric History of the Past 420,000 years from the Vostok Ice Core, Antarctica." *Nature* 399 (1999): 429–36.

———. "Vostok Ice Core Data for 420,000 Years." NOAA/NGDC Paleoclimatology Program, Boulder CO, USA. 2001. Available online at ftp://ftp .ncdc.noaa.gov/pub/data/paleo/icecore/antarctica/vostok/deutnat.txt.

Raupach, M., et al. "Global and Regional Drivers of Accelerating CO_2 Emissions." *Proceedings of the National Academy of Science* 104:24 (2007): 10288–93.

Stenni, B., et al. "EPICA Dome C Stable Isotope Data to 44.8 KYrBP." NOAA/NCDC Paleoclimatology Program, Boulder CO, USA. 2006. Available online at ftp://ftp.ncdc.noaa.gov/pub/data/paleo/icecore/ antarctica/epica_domec/edc96-iso-45kyr.txt.

Stott, L. D., et al. "Decline of Surface Temperature and Salinity in the Western Tropical Pacific Ocean in the Holocene Epoch." *Nature* 431 (2004): 56–59.

———. "Western Tropical Pacific Holocene Sea Surface Temperature and Salinity Reconstructions." NOAA/NGDC Paleoclimatology Program, Boulder CO, USA. 2004. Available online at ftp://ftp.ncdc.noaa.gov/ pub/data/paleo/contributions_by_author/stott2004/stott2004.txt.

Van Aardenne, J. A., F. Dentener, J. G. J. Olivier, and J. A. H. W. Peters. "The EDGAR 3.2 Fast Track 2000 Dataset (32FT2000)." 2005. Available online at http://www.mnp.nl/edgar/Images/Description_of _EDGAR_32FT2000(v8)_tcm32-22222.pdf.

Zhao, M., et al. "Eastern Tropical Atlantic Alkenones and Sea Surface Temperatures." NOAA/NGDC Paleoclimatology Program, Boulder, CO, USA. 2004. Available online at ftp://ftp.ncdc.noaa.gov/pub/data/ paleo/contributions_by_author/zhao1995/zhao1995.txt.

———. "Molecular Stratigraphy of Cores off Northwest Africa: Sea Surface Temperature History over the Last 80 Ka." *Paleoceanography* 10:3 (1995): 661–75.

ABOUT THE AUTHORS

KATHARINE HAYHOE is a research professor in the department of geosciences at Texas Tech University. She has degrees in physics and astronomy from the University of Toronto, and in atmospheric sciences from the University of Illinois.

Her research is motivated by the desire to communicate the reality of climate change to those who will be most affected by it. For that reason, Katharine's studies look at how climate change will affect areas as diverse as California's grape-growing regions to the city of Chicago's roads and buildings. She has led regional climate assessments for the Great Lakes region, the state of California, the U.S. Northeast, and the Midwest and served on review panels for the California Bay-Delta Authority, the International Joint Commission on the Great Lakes, and the National Oceanic and Atmospheric Administration. Katharine is a lead author for the 2009 State of Knowledge report, a federal assessment of climate change impacts on public health, water resources, energy, agriculture, and the natural environment of the United States.

Katharine also heads a scientific consulting firm, ATMOS Research and Consulting (ARC). ARC provides climate change projections and impact assessments for a broad range of industry and government clients that include city, state, and federal government agencies, nonprofit organizations, financial investment firms, and even international embassies.

Katharine is honored to have contributed her research to and served as an expert reviewer for the Intergovernmental Panel on

Climate Change, which was awarded the Nobel Peace Prize in 2007.

ANDREW FARLEY served as a professor at University of Notre Dame for five years and is now a tenured professor at Texas Tech University. He holds a bachelor's degree from Furman University, a master's degree from the University of Georgia, and a PhD from the University of Illinois at Urbana-Champaign.

Andrew offers courses in second language acquisition and an Honors College seminar course titled "Early Church and Contemporary Christianity in Conflict." Andrew has received teaching excellence awards or recognitions from three different universities. He has authored or coauthored more than a dozen peer-reviewed journal articles and three textbooks published by McGraw-Hill Higher Education. In addition, Andrew is the author of the Christian living book, *The Naked Gospel: The Truth You May Never Hear in Church* (Zondervan, 2009).

Andrew serves as the lead teaching pastor of Ecclesia (www .EcclesiaOnline.com), a growing evangelical church that has resided on the South Plains of Texas for more than fifty years. He also cohosts *Real Life in Christ*, a television program that airs every week on ABC-TV in West Texas and New Mexico.

Andrew enjoys helping Christians grow deeper in their understanding of the radical and life-changing truths of the gospel message, the birthright of every child of God.